MW01014210

When Someone Dies
IN TEXAS

ALL THE LEGAL AND PRACTICAL THINGS
YOU NEED TO DO
WHEN SOMEONE NEAR TO YOU DIES
IN THE STATE OF TEXAS

By AMELIA E. POHL, Attorney at Law

with Texas attorney
PAUL PREMACK
as consulting counsel

and
BARBARA J. SIMMONDS, Ph.D.
as consulting psychologist

 EAGLE PUBLISHING COMPANY OF BOCA

Copyright © 2000 by AMELIA E. POHL
All rights reserved.
No part of this book may be reproduced or transmitted for any purpose, in any form and by any means, graphic, electronic or mechanical, including photocopying, recording, or by any information storage or retrieval system, without permission in writing from AMELIA E. POHL.

The purpose of this book is to provide the reader with an accurate and informative overview of the subject but laws change frequently and are subject to different interpretations as courts rule on the meaning or effect of a law. This book is sold with the understanding that neither the publisher nor the authors are engaging in, nor rendering legal, medical, psychiatric, accounting or any other professional service. If you need legal, accounting, medical, psychiatric or other expert advice, then you should seek the services of a duly licensed professional.

This book is intended for use by the consumer for his or her own benefit. If you use this book to counsel someone about the law, accounting or medicine, then that may be considered an unauthorized and illegal practice.

WEB SITES: Web sites appear throughout the book. These Web sites are offered for the convenience of the reader only. Publication of these Web site addresses is not an endorsement by the authors, editors or publishers of this book.

EAGLE PUBLISHING COMPANY OF BOCA
4199 N. Dixie Highway, #2
Boca Raton, FL   33431
E-mail   info@eaglepublishing.com

Printed in the United States of America
ISBN 1-892407-17-5   PERFECT BOUND
ISBN 1-892407-16-7   CASE BOUND
Library of Congress Catalog Card Number: 00-100116

About the Author

Before becoming an attorney in 1985, AMELIA E. POHL taught mathematics on both the high school and college level. During her tenure as Associate Professor of Mathematics at Prince George's Community College in Maryland, she wrote several books including Probability: A Set Theory Approach, Principals of Counting and Common Stock Sense.

During her practice of law Attorney Pohl observed that many people want to reduce the high cost of legal fees by performing or assisting with their own legal transactions. Attorney Pohl found that, with a bit of guidance, people are able to perform many legal transactions for themselves. Attorney Pohl is utilizing her background as teacher, author and attorney to provide that "bit of guidance" to the general public in the form of self-help legal books that she has written. Attorney Pohl is currently working on "translating" this book for the rest of the states:

When Someone Dies In Arkansas

When Someone Dies in Connecticut, etc.

Consulting Texas Attorney

Attorney PAUL PREMACK has been in private legal practice since 1983 focusing on Elder Law. He and his wife Ruthie, and their two children, live in San Antonio, Texas. Paul is a graduate of he University of Texas at Austin and the University of Houston College of Law. He is certified as a Geriatric Scholar by the University of Texas Health Science Center in San Antonio.

Paul Premack writes a newspaper column focusing on legal issues faced by the senior community. It appears in the San Antonio Express-News and the Austin Senior Advocate. He is published in the Texas Bar Journal, is the co-author of the book Texas Elder Law: The Basics and Beyond, and is the author of the Senior Texan Legal Guide, now in its third edition.

Many of Paul's legal writings are available over the Internet. The web site address is www.Premack.com. His web site has several cutting edge innovations designed to make legal services affordable and accessible to the Senior community — including an on-line legal consultation service, and on-line legal forms, including most of the forms discussed later in this book.

Paul is a member of the National Academy of Elder Law Attorneys. He was President of Guardianship Services in 1998-1999, and is a former member of the Advisory Board to the Alamo Area Agency on Aging. He is on the Board of the Elder Information Library. He was Chair of the First Annual People's Law School, co-sponsored by the San Antonio Bar Foundation and by St. Mary's University Law School.

Consulting Psychologist

BARBARA J. SIMMONDS, Ph.D., a noted psychologist, has collaborated with the author on those sections of this book dealing with the grieving process. Dr. Simmonds has been practicing in the field of Health/Rehabilitation Psychology and Gerontology for the past 10 years. Her experiences in the field led her as a natural outcome to develop expertise also in Grief Counseling, since so many losses accrue to individuals in a health care setting.

In addition to her work in hospitals, nursing centers and private practice, Dr. Simmonds has served as Adjunct Faculty at Nova Southeastern University, teaching courses in Aging, Stress Management and Grief Counseling. Dr. Simmonds holds a Master's Degree in Gerontology and a Ph.D. in Clinical Psychology from Nova Southeastern University. She was the Director of Psychological Services at Villa Maria Nursing and Rehabilitation Center for eight years and now continues her relationship with the institution on a consultation basis. She continues with her private practice in North Miami, Florida.

To my brother, Paul Adinolfi,
his intelligence, good humor and kindness,
his strength during our times of family loss,
have set the beacon standard for me to follow.

ACKNOWLEDGMENT

When someone dies, the family attorney is often among the first to be called. Family members have questions about whether probate is necessary, who to notify, how to get possession of the assets, etc. Over the years, as we practiced in the field of Elder Law, we noticed that the questions raised were much the same family to family. We both agreed that a book answering such questions would be of service to the general public. We wish to thank all of the clients, whom we have had the honor and pleasure to serve, for providing us with the impetus to produce this book.

Special thanks from AMELIA E. POHL
I wish to express my sincere appreciation for the assistance and encouragement given to me by Martha Dermer, Michael J. DeMarie, CPA, my daughters Louise Lucas and Margot Bosche, and to my husband J. William Pohl.

Special thanks from PAUL PREMACK
My sincere thanks to my wife Ruthie S. Premack and to our children Tiffany and Benjamin. And to all my clients who through years of joy and travail, have helped me become a better elder attorney.

When Someone Dies in Texas

CONTENTS

About this book

We have tried to make this book as comprehensive as possible so there are specialized sections of the book that do not apply to the general population and may not be of interest to you. The following GUIDE POSTS appear throughout the book. You can read the section if the situation applies to you or skip the section if it doesn't.

GUIDE POSTS

 The SPOUSE POST means that the information provided is specifically for the spouse of the decedent. If the decedent was single, then skip this section.

 The CALL-A-LAWYER POST alerts you to a situation that may require the assistance of an attorney. See page xiv for suggestions about how to find a lawyer.

 The CAUTION POST alerts you to a potential problem. It is followed by a suggestion about how to avoid the problem.

 The SPECIAL SITUATION POST means that the information given in that paragraph applies to a particular event or situation; for example when the decedent dies a violent death. If the situation does not apply in your case, then you can skip the section.

The Organization of the Book

There are six steps in settling the estate of the decedent:

1. Tending to the funeral and burial
2. Telling everyone that the person died
3. Locating all of the decedent's property
4. Paying any outstanding bills
5. Determining who are the beneficiaries
6. Getting the decedent's property to the proper beneficiary

We devoted a chapter to each of these 6 steps (see the table of contents). We placed a CHECK LIST at the end of Chapter 6 to assist you in remembering things that need to be done.

Chapters 1 through 6 identify problems that can occur when someone dies. Chapters 7 and 8 explain how to set up your own estate plan so that your family is not burdened by similar problems.

Chapter 9 offers suggestions that may help if you are having difficulty getting through the grieving process.

GLOSSARY

This book is designed for the average reader. Legal terminology has been kept to a minimum. There is a glossary at the end of the book in the event you come across a legal term that is not familiar to you.

FICTITIOUS NAMES AND EVENTS

The examples in this book are based loosely on actual events; however, all names are fictitious and the events as portrayed, are fictitious.

Reading the Law

Where applicable, we identified the state statute or federal statute that is the basis of the discussion. We did this as a reference, but also to encourage the general public to read the law as it is written. Prior to the Internet the only way you could look up the law was to physically take yourself to the local courthouse law library or the law section of a public library. Today all of the state and federal statutes are literally at your finger tips. They are just a mouse click away on the Internet. All you need to look up the law is the address of the web site and the identifying number of the statute:

TEXAS STATUTE WEB SITE
http://capitol.tlc.state.tx.us/statutes/statutes.html
FEDERAL STATUTE WEB SITE
http://www4.law.cornell.edu/uscode

Texas 27 different codes, including BUSINESS CORPORATION ACT, CIVIL PRACTICE & REMEDIES, PROBATE, INSURANCE, HEALTH & SAFETY, FAMILY, PROPERTY, etc. Each Code is divided into Chapters and each Chapter into sections. The notation (FAMILY 2.501) refers to Chapter 2, Section 501 of the Family Code. To find this law, all you need do is go to the web site, look up FAMILY CODE, then go to section 2.501.

If you come across a topic that is of importance to you, then you may find it both interesting and profitable to actually read the law as written.

When You Need A Lawyer

This book describes Texas law as in effect when the book was written. We pay our legislators (state and federal) to make laws and, if necessary, change those in effect. We pay judges to interpret the law and that interpretation may change the way the law operates. The legislature and the judiciary do their job and so laws change frequently.

The purpose of the book is to give the reader an overview of what needs to be done when someone dies, and to provide information about how a person can arrange his own affairs to avoid problems for his own family. It is not intended as a substitute for legal counsel or any other kind of professional advice. If you have any legal question, then you should seek the counsel of an attorney. When looking for an attorney, consider three things: EXPERTISE, COST and PERSONALITY.

EXPERTISE
The State of Texas has legal specialist programs for fourteen areas of practice including Administrative Law; Civil trial; Immigration; Tax; Estate Planning and Probate. To be a *certified specialist* the attorney must pass a written examination, demonstrate a high level of experience in the field, be favorably evaluated by other attorneys and judges familiar with their work and fulfill ongoing education requirements. You can call the Lawyer Referral Information Service for information about how to reach an attorney who practices in the area of law that you seek by calling (800) 252-9690. The State Bar of Texas has a web site that lists certified Lawyer Referral Services:

 THE STATE BAR OF TEXAS WEB SITE
http://www.texasbar.com

Certification is just one of the criteria to consider. Many fine attorneys are experienced in an area of law, but have not taken the time, effort and expense to become certified as a specialist in that area of law by the Texas Bar. If the attorney is not certified in the branch of law that you need, then ask how long he has practiced that type of law and what percentage of his practice is devoted to that type of law.

Of course, the best way to find an attorney, is through personal referral. Ask your friends, family or business acquaintances if they have used an attorney for the field of law that you seek and whether they were pleased with the results. It is important to employ an attorney who is experienced in the kind of law you seek. Your friend may have had a wonderful Estate Planning attorney, but if you have suffered an injury, then you need a Personal Injury attorney.

COST

In addition to the attorney's experience, it is important to check out his/her fees. When you call for an appointment ask what the attorney will charge for the initial consultation and the approximate cost for the service you seek. Ask whether there will be any additional costs such as filing fees, accounting fees, expert witness fees, etc. If the least expensive attorney is out of your price range then there are many state and private agencies throughout the state that provide legal assistance for people of low income. You can look up the nearest Legal Service in your telephone directory, or you can call the local Bar Association for the telephone number of the local Pro Bono Organization. The American Bar Association has a web site that lists telephone numbers for Pro Bono Programs:

AMERICAN BAR ASSOCIATION WEB SITE
http://www.abanet.org/legalservices/probono/pb-texas.html

PERSONALITY

Of equal importance to the attorney's experience and legal fees, is your relationship with the attorney. How easy was it to reach the attorney? Did you go through layers of receptionists and legal assistants before being allowed to speak to the attorney? Did the attorney promptly return your call? If you had difficulty reaching the attorney, then you can expect similar problems should you employ that attorney.

Did the attorney treat you with respect? Did the attorney treat you paternally with a "father knows best" attitude or did the attorney treat you as an intelligent person with the ability to understand the options available to you and the ability to make your own decision based on the information provided to you.

Are you able to understand and easily communicate with the attorney? Is he/she speaking to you in plain English or is his/her explanation of the matter so full of legalese to be almost meaningless to you?

Do you find the attorney's personality to be pleasant or grating? Sometimes people rub each other the wrong way. It is like rubbing a cat the wrong way. Stroking a cat from head to tail is pleasing to the cat, but petting it in the opposite direction, no matter how well intended, causes friction. If the lawyer makes you feel annoyed or uncomfortable then find another attorney.

It is worth the effort to take the time to interview as many attorneys as it takes to find one with the right expertise, fee schedule and personality for you.

The First Week 1

Dealing with the death of a close family member or friend is difficult. Not only do you need to deal with your own emotions, but often with those of your family and friends. Sometimes their sorrow is more painful to you, than what you are experiencing yourself.

In addition to the emotional impact of a death, there are many things that need to be done, from arranging the funeral and burial, to closing out the business affairs of the decedent, and finally giving whatever property is left to the proper beneficiary.

The funeral and burial take only a few days. Wrapping up the affairs of the decedent may take considerably longer. This chapter explains what things you (the spouse or closest family member) need to do during the first week, beginning at the moment of death and continuing through the funeral.

 MALE GENDER USED

Rather than use "he/she" or "his/her" for simplicity
(and hoping not to offend anyone)
we will refer to the decedent using the male gender.

References to other people will be in both genders.

AUTOPSIES

Years ago people died natural deaths from unknown causes. Doctors often requested permission from family members to perform autopsies to determine the cause of death. In today's high tech world of medicine, doctors are fairly certain of the cause of death, but if there is a question, the family may be asked for permission to perform an autopsy. Texas statute (Crim. Proc. 49.13) gives an order of priority for the person authorized to sign:

1st   the spouse   2nd   an adult child of the decedent
3rd   the legal guardian of decedent's child
4th   a parent   5th   the decedent's guardian
6th   a next of kin

If none of these are available, then anyone who assumes responsibility to bury the body can authorize the autopsy.

The cost of an autopsy runs anywhere from $2,500 to $3,500. The person giving authorization must agree to pay for the autopsy because the cost is not covered under most health insurance plans.   It is in the family's best interest to consent to the autopsy because such examination might reveal a genetic disorder, that could be treated if it later appears in another family member. Even if no such disease is found, knowing the cause of death with certainty is better than not knowing.

An example that comes to mind is a woman who was taken to the hospital complaining of stomach pains. The doctors diagnosed her as suffering from gallbladder disease, but she died before they could effectively treat her. A doctor suggested that an autopsy be performed to determine the actual cause of death.   The woman had three daughters, one of whom objected to the autopsy:

> "Why spend that kind of money?
> It won't bring Mom back."

The daughter's wishes were respected, however over the years as they aged and became ill with their own various ailments they would undergo physical examinations. As part of taking their medical history, doctors routinely asked "And what was the cause of your mother's death?" None could answer the question.

This is not a dramatic story. No mysterious genetic disorder ever occurred in any of her daughters, nor in any of their children. But each daughter (including the one who objected) at some point in her life, was confronted with the nagging question "What did Mom die of?"

MANDATORY AUTOPSIES

When a person dies, a physician must sign the death certificate stating the cause of death. If a person dies in a hospital, then there is a doctor present to sign the certificate. If a person dies at home from natural causes or any other reason (accident, violence, suicide) then the police must be notified. The person who discovers the body should call 911 to summon the police. The police will ask the Medical Examiner to determine the cause of death. If there is a suspicion that the death was not from natural causes or if the decedent died from a disease that might pose a threat to the public health, then the Medical Examiner will either perform or order an autopsy (Health & Safety 81.045 and Crim. Proc. 49.13 (b)).

AUTOPSIES PERFORMED BY THE INSURANCE COMPANY

A company that issues accident and sickness insurance in the state of Texas is required to include a provision in their policy stating that the company has the right to perform an autopsy (Insurance 3.70-3 A(10). The cost of the autopsy is paid for by the insurance company, so they will not order an autopsy unless there is some important reason to do so.

ANATOMICAL GIFTS

If, before death, the decedent made an anatomical gift by signing a donor card then hospital personnel or the donor's doctor needs to be made aware of the gift in quick proximity to the time of death — preferably before death.

GIFT AUTHORIZED BY THE FAMILY
Hospital personnel determine whether a mortally ill patient is a candidate for an organ donation. Early on in the donor program those over 65 were not considered as suitable candidates. Today, however, the condition of the organ, and not the age, is the determining factor.

The federal government has established regional Organ Procurement Organizations throughout the United States to coordinate the donor program. There are Organ Procurement Organizations located in Dallas (Southwest Transplant Alliance), San Antonio (Texas Organ Sharing Alliance) and Houston (LifeGift Organ Donation Center). If it is decided that the patient is a candidate, the hospital will contact the local Organ Procurement Organization.

The Organ Procurement Organization will determine whether the patient is a suitable donor. If they decide to request the gift and the candidate did not sign a donor card then someone in the family must give written permission. Someone who is specially trained will approach the family to request the donation. Texas statute (Health & Safety 692.004) establishes an order of priority to authorize the donation:

> 1st The spouse
> 2nd The decedent's adult child
> 3rd Either of the decedent's parents
> 4th An adult brother or sister
> 5th A court appointed guardian (if any)
> 6th Anyone else authorized to dispose of the body

If permission is obtained from a family member and there are others in the same or a higher priority, then an effort must be made to contact those people and make them aware of the proposed gift. For example, if the brother of the decedent agrees to the gift (4th in priority) and the decedent had an adult son (2nd in priority) then the son should be made aware of the gift. If the son objects, then no gift can be made. Similarly, the statute prohibits the gift if the decedent ever expressed his opposition to a donation.

AFTER THE DONATION

Once the donation is made the body is delivered to the funeral home and prepared for burial or cremation as directed by the family. The donation does not disfigure the body so there can be an open casket viewing if the family so wishes.

Some regional Organ Procurement Organizations have an aftercare program that includes a letter of condolence to the family and an expression of gratitude for the gift. For privacy reasons, the identity of the recipient of the gift is not disclosed, but on request from the family, the local Organ Procurement Organization will give the family basic demographic information about the donation, such as the age, sex, marital status, number of children and occupation of the recipient of the gift.

GIFT FOR EDUCATION OR RESEARCH

If the decedent signed a donor card indicating his wish to use his body for any purpose and he is not a candidate for an organ donation, then you can offer to release the body for study or research to a school of medicine or university, such as:

Texas A & M University   (409) 845-4913
College of Medicine, Department of Anatomy
College Station, TX   77843

University of Texas   (817) 735-2048
Health Science Center, Department of Anatomy
Ft. Worth, TX   76107

University of Texas   (409) 772-1293
Medical Branch at Galveston
Galveston, TX 77550

Texas Tech University   (806) 743-2700
School of Medicine, Department of Anatomy
Lubbock, TX   79430

You will need to call the school to determine whether they will accept the body. Most schools will not accept bodies from those who have died from a contagious disease or from crushing injuries. If they agree to accept the body then you need to inquire whether there will be any cost to transport or bury the body. Most universities cover the cost of transporting the body to the university from a local area. The study usually takes from 18 month to 2 years. Once the project is complete the remains are cremated. Most universities give families the choice of having the *cremains* (cremated remains) returned to the family or buried at a local cemetery.

THE FUNERAL

Approximately one third of the population dies suddenly from an accident or undetected illness. Two thirds of the population die after being ill for a year or more with the most common scenario being that of an aged person dying after being ill for several months. In such cases, the death is expected. Family and friends are emotionally prepared for the happening. Whether expected or unexpected, the first job is the disposition of the body.

THE PREARRANGED FUNERAL

Increasingly, people are arranging, in advance, for their own funeral and burial. This makes it easier on the family both financially and emotionally. All the decisions have been made and there is no guessing what the decedent would have wanted.

If the decedent made provision for his burial space, then you need to locate the burial certificate. If the decedent purchased a preneed funeral plan, then you need to locate the contract. You should read the contract to determine what provisions were made. Some contracts are paid on an installment basis. If the decedent signed such a contract, then you need to find out what monies were paid and whether there is a remaining balance due.

If you cannot locate the contract, but you know the name of the funeral home, then call and ask them to send you a copy of the contract. If you believe the decedent purchased a funeral plan but you do not know the name of the funeral home, then call the local funeral homes. Many local funeral homes are owned by national firms with computer capacity to identify people who have purchased a contract in any of their many locations.

Once you have possession of the contract, bring it with you to the funeral home and go over the terms of the contract with the funeral director. Inquire whether there is any charge that is not included in the contract.

MAKING FUNERAL ARRANGEMENTS

If the decedent died unexpectedly or without having made any prior funeral arrangements then your first job is to chose a funeral director and make arrangements for the funeral or cremation. Most people choose the nearest or most conveniently located funeral home without comparison shopping, however prices for these services can vary significantly from funeral home to funeral home. Savings can be had if you take the time to make a few phone calls.

Receiving price quotes by telephone is your right under Texas law (Rev. Civ. Stat. 4582(b)). This statute requires a funeral director to give general price information by telephone within a reasonable time. Funeral homes are listed in the telephone directory under FUNERAL DIRECTORS. If you live in a small town, there may be only one or two listings. If such is the case, then check out some funeral homes in the next largest city.

Funeral Directors usually provide the following services:
➢ arrange for the transportation of the body
  to the funeral home and then to the burial site
➢ obtain burial transit permits
➢ arrange for the embalming or cremation of the body
➢ arrange funeral and memorial services
➢ arrange to have the obituary printed
➢ order copies of the death certificate for the family
➢ have acknowledgment and prayer cards printed.

To compare prices you will need to determine:

✧ what is included in the price of a basic funeral plan

✧ whether you can expect any additional cost.

If the decedent did not own a burial space, then that cost must be included when making funeral arrangements. Embalming may be necessary if you are going to have a viewing. Embalming is not necessary if you order a direct cremation or an immediate burial. Both state and federal law prohibit any charge for embalming, or any other service, unless you order that service (Rev. Civ. Stat. 4582b (H)(11a), Federal Trade Commission Rule 453.5).

PURCHASING THE CASKET

When comparison-shopping, you will find that the single most expensive item in the funeral arrangement is the casket. Most funeral directors will quote you a price for the basic funeral plan. That plan does not include the cost of the casket. Directors usually quote a range of prices for the casket, saying that you will need to come in and choose the casket at the time you contract for the funeral. When selecting a casket you should be aware that there is often a considerable markup in the price quoted by the funeral director. You do not need to deal "sole source" in the purchase of the casket. You can purchase a casket elsewhere and have it delivered to the funeral home for use instead of the one offered by the funeral director.

In 1994, The Federal Trade Commission ("FTC") ruled that funeral homes had to accept caskets purchased elsewhere. (FTC Rule 453.4) The FTC ruling includes a ban on funeral homes charging a handling fee for accepting a casket purchased elsewhere. Since that ruling the retail casket business has increased significantly. Retail stores that sell caskets have opened in California and New York. As retail casket sales increase funeral directors will begin to price their caskets competitively with the retail casket sales market — all to the benefit of the consumer.

If you wish to shop for a casket, then the best time to do so is before you go to the funeral home to arrange for the funeral. You can find a retail casket sales outlet in the telephone book under CASKETS. You may need to look in the telephone directory for the nearest large city to find a listing. For users of the Internet, you can use your search engine to find the retail sales casket company nearest you. By making a call to a retail casket sales dealer, you will become knowledgeable in the price range of caskets. You can then decide what is a reasonable price for the product you seek.

Once you have determined what you should pay for the casket, it is only fair to give the funeral director the opportunity to meet that price. If you cannot reach a meeting of the minds, then you can always order the casket from the retail sales dealer and have it delivered to the funeral home.

OTHER ON-LINE FUNERAL SERVICES
The Internet is changing the way the world does business, and the funeral industry is no exception. A growing number of mortuaries are offering live Webcasts of funerals and wakes for those who are unable to pay their respects in person.

There are Web sites that offer online memorials, obituary notices as well as online eulogies and testimonials. There is even a Web site that offers a posthumous e-mail service which allows people to leave final messages for friends and relatives.

THE CREMATION

Increasingly people are opting for cremation. The reasons for choosing cremation are varied, but for the majority, it is a matter of finances. The cost of cremation is approximately one-sixth that of an ordinary funeral and burial. A major saving is the cost of the casket. No casket is necessary for the cremation. Federal law prohibits a Funeral Director from saying that a casket is required for a direct cremation (FTC Rule 453.3 (b)ii). If you want to have a viewing of the body and/or a funeral service with the body present, then you can arrange to rent a casket from the Funeral Director for the service.

If you are having a memorial service in a place of worship with no viewing of the body before the cremation, then consider contracting with a facility that does cremations only. Look in the telephone book CREMATION SERVICES. You will also see cremation "societies" in the telephone book. Some are for-profit and others not-for-profit. You can also find advertisements for cremation services on the Internet.

These cremation facilities provide much the same services as a funeral home but with one important exception — the cremation service does not provide any type of funeral service or public viewing of the body.

 *Special Situation* THE OVERWEIGHT DECEDENT

If the decedent weighs more than 300 pounds, then you need to check to see if the Cremation service has facilities large enough to handle the body. If you cannot locate a crematory that can accommodate the body, then you will need to make burial arrangements.

DISPOSING OF THE ASHES

The decedent's cremains can be place in a cemetery. Many cemeteries have a separate building called a *columbarium*, which is a building especially designed to store urns. If not, then the cremains can be placed in a cemetery plot. Some cemeteries allow the cremains of a family member to be placed in a occupied family plot. Similarly, some cemeteries will allow the cremains to be place in the space in a mausoleum that is currently occupied by a member of the decedent's family. If it is your desire to have the cremains placed in an occupied family plot or mausoleum, then you need to call the cemetery and ask them to explain their policy as it relates to the burial of urns in occupied sites.

If the cremains are to be placed in a cemetery, then you need to obtain a suitable urn for the burial. You can purchase the urn from the Funeral Director or Crematory Service Director. Urns cost much less than caskets, but they can cost several hundred dollars. You may wish to do some comparison shopping by calling a retail sales casket dealer.

The decedent may have expressed a desire that his ashes be spread out to sea. The Funeral Director or Cremation Service Director can assist you with such arrangements.

If the decedent is to be buried in another state, then the body will need to be transported to that state. Most funeral homes belong to a national network of funeral homes, and the out-of-state Funeral Director has the means to make local arrangements to ship the body. Contact the out-of-state Funeral Director and have him/her make arrangement with the airline for the transportation of the body.

If services are to be held in Texas and in another state, then contact the local funeral director and he will make arrangements with the out-of-state funeral home for the transportation of the body.

If the body has been cremated, then you can transport the cremains yourself, either by carrying the ashes as part of your luggage or by arranging with the airline to transport the ashes as cargo. Have a certified copy of the death certificate available in the event that you need to identify the remains of the decedent. Call the airline before departure and ask whether they have any special regulation or procedure regarding the transportation of human ashes.

| SPOUSE | ➤ | THE MILITARY BURIAL |

Subject to availability of burial spaces, an honorably discharged veteran and/or his unmarried minor or handicapped child and/or his un-remarried spouse may be buried in a national military cemetery. Some cemeteries, such as the Fort Sam Houston National Cemetery and the Kerrville National Cemetery, have room only for cremated remains or for the casketed remains of a family member of someone who is currently buried in that cemetery, so you will need to call for space availability.

There are six national military cemeteries in Texas and another scheduled to open at Dallas:

Fort Bliss National Cemetery	(915) 564-0201
Fort Sam Houston National Cemetery	(210) 820-3891
Houston National Cemetery	(281) 447-8686
Kerrville National Cemetery	(210) 820-3891
San Antonio National Cemetery	(210) 820-3891
Dallas-Fort Worth National Cemetery	(214) 467-3374

The Dallas-Fort Worth National Cemetery has been under development for several years and is scheduled to begin burials in the year 2000.

The Department of the Army is in charge of the Arlington National Cemetery. If you wish to have an eligible deceased veteran buried in the Arlington National Cemetery, then call them at (703) 695-3250.

Arlington National Cemetery
Interment Service Branch
Arlington, VA 22211

Special Situation

THE COST OF A MILITARY BURIAL

Burial space in a National Cemetery is free of charge. Cemetery employees will open and close the grave and mark it with headstone or grave marker without cost to the family. The local Veteran's Administration ("VA") will provide the family with a memorial flag. The family needs to make funeral arrangements with a funeral firm and have them transport the remains to the cemetery.

If the decedent was receiving a VA pension then the VA will pay a burial and funeral expense allowance regardless of where the veteran is buried. The VA will not reimburse any burial or funeral cost for the spouse of a veteran.

For information about reimbursement of funeral and burial expenses you can call the VA:
(800)-827-1000.

The Department of Veteran's Affairs has a web site with information on the following topics:

- ➢ National and Military Cemeteries
- ➢ Burial, Headstones and Markers
- ➢ State Cemetery Grants Program
- ➢ Obtaining Military Records
- ➢ Locating Veterans

 VA CEMETERY WEB SITE
http://www.cem.va.gov

 **SPOUSE** → # BENEFITS FOR SPOUSE OF DECEDENT VETERAN

If the decedent was honorably discharged, then regardless of where he is buried, his spouse might be eligible for a contribution from the Veteran's Administration for his funeral and burial expenses. If the decedent had minor or disabled children, his spouse may also be eligible for a monthly benefit of Dependency and Indemnity Compensation ("DIC").

If the Veteran's surviving spouse receives nursing home care under Medicaid, then the spouse might be eligible for a monthly payment from the VA. Whether the surviving spouse is eligible for any of these benefits depends on many factors including whether the decedent was serving on active duty, whether his death was service related, and the surviving spouse's assets and income.

For information about whether the surviving spouse is eligible for any benefit related to the decedent's military service, call the VETERANS ADMINISTRATION at (800) 827-1000.

You can receive a printed statement of public policy: VA Pamphlet 051-000-00217-2 FEDERAL BENEFITS FOR VETERANS AND DEPENDENTS by sending a check in the amount of $5 to: THE SUPERINTENDENT OF DOCUMENT
P.O. Box 371954
Pittsburgh, PA 15250-7954

Information is also available on the VA web site:

VA WEB SITE
http://www.va.gov

| Special Situation | THE PROBLEM FUNERAL OR BURIAL |

The funeral and burial industry is well regulated by the state and federal government. Under Texas statute (Rev. Civil Stat. 4582(b)) the following acts are subject to disciplinary action:

⊠ Delivering goods of a lesser quality than that presented to the purchaser as a sample

⊠ Using a false or misleading advertisement

⊠ Stating or implying that the customer's concern for cost shows a lack of respect for the decedent

⊠ Failing to provide a customer with a price list at the beginning of the discussion

⊠ Being unfit because of a substance abuse

Funeral directors are licensed professionals so it is unusual to have a problem with the funeral or burial or cremation. If, however, you had a bad experience with any aspect of the funeral then you can file a complaint with the state licensing agency:

Texas Funeral Service Commission
510 S. Congress, Suite 206
Austin, TX 78704-1716
Telephone (512) 479-7222

 **LAWYER** If you are not satisfied with the results obtained, then consult with an attorney who is experienced in litigation matters.

THE VIOLENT DEATH

Special Situation

If the decedent died a violent death or under circumstances in which foul play is suspected, the Medical Examiner will take possession of the body. The body will not be released to the funeral director until the examination of the body is complete. In the interim, the family can proceed with arrangements for the funeral. The funeral director will contact the Medical Examiner to determine when he can pick up the body and proceed with the funeral.

THE ACCIDENTAL OR CRIMINAL DEATH

 **LAWYER**

If the decedent died because of an accident then it is important to contact a Personal Injury attorney to determine whether the family has a case for wrongful death. If the accident was related to the decedent's job, the family may wish to consult with a Worker's Compensation attorney as well.

If the decedent died because of a criminal act and you are a family member, then you may wish to contact an attorney experienced in Criminal Law to learn of your rights as a family member.

Special Situation ▷ CRIME VICTIM COMPENSATION

If the decedent died because of a criminal act and you are a family member then you may be eligible to receive compensation under the **TEXAS CRIME VICTIMS COMPENSATION ACT**. If there are no other resources available (such as health or life insurance), the state can assist with funeral or medical expenses, psychiatric counseling, care of a dependent, etc. up to a maximum of $50,000.

There are certain criteria that must be met, such as, the victim must be innocent of the crime, the crime was reported within a reasonable period of time and there was cooperation with the authorities. You need to file the application within 3 years from the date of the crime. You can get an application from the prosecutor's office or you can call (800) 983-9933. In Austin, call (512) 936-1200. You can download an application form from the Internet:

 TEXAS CRIME VICTIM SERVICES
http://www.oag.state.tx.us/victims/victims.htm

The Texas Attorney General will conduct an investigation to determine eligibility. The process may take several weeks. If the Attorney General determines that emergency funds are needed (for example, to pay for the burial) then he can release up to $1,500. What ever amount is awarded as emergency funds is deducted from the final award.

You can be represented by an attorney. The state will pay for attorney's fees up to 25% of whatever amount is awarded. It is unlawful for the attorney to receive any money in excess of the 25% paid by the state (Crim. Proced. 56.31, 56.37, 56.42, 56.43, 56.46, 56.50).

THE UNCLAIMED BODY

The Commissioners Court of each county provides for the burial or cremation of unidentified bodies and those who die without funds. If an indigent person dies and the police can identify the body, they will try to locate the family. If the decedent was an honorably discharged veteran, then the Veteran's Administration will arrange for a burial. If the decedent was not an honorable discharged veteran and his family is unable (or unwilling) to make burial arrangements, then the county will provide for his interment or cremation. If the county decides on cremation and a family member or friend of the decedent objects to the procedure, then the county will have the decedent buried (Health & Safety 694.002).

The state of Texas has created an Anatomical Board to coordinate donations to medical schools for the advancement of medical science. If a body is unclaimed, then before the county buries or cremates the body, they must notify the Anatomical Board of the State of Texas. The Board may decide to have the body donated to a medical school. If they do, then the relatives of the decedent have 60 days after the body is delivered to the medical school to claim the body. If a relative claims the body, it will be released to him/her without any charge.

If the unclaimed body is identified as that of a traveler, the Board will require the institution receiving the body, to keep it for 6 months for the purposes of identification. (Health & Safety 691.023, 691.025, 691.026).

☎ LAWYER   THE MISSING BODY

Few things are more difficult to deal with than a missing person. The emotional turmoil created by the "not knowing" is often more difficult than the finality of death. The legal problems created by the disappearance are also more difficult than if the person simply died. It may take a two-part legal process — an initial guardianship procedure to handle the missing person's affairs while he is missing and then a final probate procedure if he is later declared dead or found dead:

BEGINNING THE PROBATE PROCEDURE
If the circumstances of the disappearance are sufficient to justify the belief that the missing person is dead then the family can begin a probate procedure. Circumstantial evidence of the death will need to be presented to the Probate court. The judge may require that law enforcement and public welfare agencies be notified of the disappearance. The court might also require that an investigative agency be hired to try to find the missing person. The cost of the search is billed to the missing person's estate.

Once the court is satisfied that there is sufficient evidence of the death, Letters will be issued to the Personal Representative and the probate procedure can begin. The court will not allow the decedent's property to be distributed to the heirs until three years from the date that the Letters were issued. If the missing person turns up after the property has been distributed, then the court will order that his property (or its cash equivalent) be returned to him (Probate Chap.V, Sec. 72).

THE DEATH CERTIFICATE

It is the job of the Funeral Director or Cremation Service Director to provide information about the decedent to the Texas Bureau of Vital Statistics. The Bureau will prepare a death certificate based on that information. It is important that the information you give to the Funeral or Cremation Director is correct. It is also important that you check the form completed by the Funeral or Cremation Director to be sure names are correctly spelled and dates correctly written. Once the information is submitted to the Bureau of Vital Statistics, it will be difficult and time consuming to make a correction.

The Funeral Director or Cremation Service Director will order as many death certificates as you request. Most establishments require an original certified copy and not a photocopy so you need to order sufficient certified copies. The following is a list of institutions that may want a certified copy as proof that the person died:

* Each insurance company that insured the decedent or his property (health insurance company, life insurance company, car insurance company, home insurance company)

* Each financial institution in which the decedent had money invested (brokerage houses, banks)

* The decedent's pension fund

* Each credit card company used by the decedent

* The IRS

* The Social Security Administration

* The title company insuring title to real property owned by the decedent and later transferred.

ORDERING COPIES OF THE DEATH CERTIFICATE

Some airlines and car rental companies offer a discount for short notice, emergency trips. If you have family flying in for the funeral, you may wish to order a few extra copies of the death certificate so that they can obtain an airline or car rental discount.

If you wish to order certified copies of the death certificate at a later date, you can call the funeral director and ask him to do so or you can order them yourself. If the death occurred in a large city, then you can order the death certificate from the city's health department:

San Antonio: Metropolitan Health District (210) 207-8780
Houston: Bureau of Vital Records   (713) 794-9069
Dallas: Bureau of Vital Statistics   (214) 670-4535

For deaths occurring outside a major metropolitan area you can write to: The Bureau of Vital Statistics
                    Department of Health
                    P.O. Box 12040
                    Austin, TX 78711-2040

You may save some time by first calling or sending an E-mail and asking what information they require.
                    Telephone: (512) 458-7111
                    E-mail: register@tdh.state.tx.us

The current cost of a death certificate is $9 for the first copy and $3 for each additional copy that is ordered at the same time. You need to make your check or money order payable to the Texas Department of Health or the city department issuing the death certificate.

RECORDING THE DEATH CERTIFICATE

In Texas, the Department of Public Health issues the death certificate. The Department does not publish the death certificate so it is not part of the public record. If the decedent owned real property in his name only or jointly with another, then when the property is transferred the title company will need a certified copy of the death certificate in order to insure the title. In many states the death certificate is recorded along with the deed of transfer; however this is not the practice in Texas.

DECEDENT WITH OUT OF STATE PROPERTY

If the decedent owned property in another state, then that state may require his death certificate be recorded in the county where that property is located. In some states the county Registrar or the Clerk of the Circuit Court is in charge of recording deeds (and death certificates). You may want to call the Clerk to determine whether a death certificate needs to be recorded in that state.

We will be discussing how to transfer real property in Chapter 6. You will find that, in many cases, you will need the assistance of an attorney to transfer the decedent's real property to the proper beneficiary. It is prudent to contact an attorney in the state where the property is located for advise about what document needs to be recorded in order to transfer the decedent's real property in that state.

About Probate

Once a person dies, all of the property he owns as of the date of his death is referred to as the *decedent's estate.* If the decedent owned property that was in his name only (not jointly or in trust for someone) then some sort of court procedure is necessary to determine who is entitled to possession of the property. The name of the court procedure is *probate.*

The root of the word probate is "to prove." It refers to the first job of the probate court, that is, to examine proof of whether the decedent *testate* (with a valid Will) or whether the decedent died *intestate* (without a Will). The second job of the probate court is to appoint someone to wrap up the affairs of the decedent — to pay any outstanding bills and then to distribute what property is left to the beneficiaries.

If the decedent named someone in his Will to be the *Executor* of his estate, then court will appoint that person for the job and issue *Letters Testamentary* giving him authority to administer the estate. If the decedent died intestate, then the court will appoint someone to be the *Administrator* of the his estate and issue *Letters of Administration.* The term *Personal Representative* is used to represent anyone who has the job of settling the decedent's estate. For simplicity we will use that term, and we will refer to the document authorizing him to act, as *Letters* (Probate Chap. I, Sec. 3 (z)(aa)).

There are different ways to conduct a probate procedure depending on the value of the probate estate and whether the decedent owned real property at the time of his death. The method of conducting a probate procedure is called the *estate administration*. Chapter 6 explains how to determine whether a probate procedure is necessary and if so, then what kind of administration is necessary.

Giving Notice Of The Death   2

Those closest to the decedent usually notify family members and close friends by telephone. The funeral director will arrange to have an obituary published in as many different newspapers as the family requests, but there is still the job of notifying the government and people who were doing business with the decedent. That task belongs to the person the decedent appointed as Executor of his Will. If the decedent died without a Will then Texas statute (Probate Chap. V, Sec. 77) gives the following order of priority for the appointment of a Personal Representative:

1. the decedent's spouse
2. the principal beneficiary of the decedent's estate
3. the next of kin
4. a creditor of the decedent
5. anyone of good character who lives in the county where the estate is being probated
6. anyone the court determines suitable for the job

If no probate procedure is necessary, the job of notifying people of the death and settling the decedent's affairs falls to his spouse; and in the absence of a spouse, to the decedent's next of kin. By *next of kin,* we mean those people who inherit the decedent's property according to the Texas Law of Intestate Succession. That law is explained in Chapter 5: TEXAS'S INTESTATE LAW.

The person who has the job of settling the decedent's estate should begin to give notice as soon as is practicable after the death. Two government agencies that need to be notified are the Social Security Administration and the IRS. This chapter gives their telephone number as well as those of all the other agencies that need to be notified.

NOTIFYING SOCIAL SECURITY

Many Funeral Directors will, as part of their service package, notify the Social Security Administration of the death. You may want to check this has been done. You can do so by calling (800) 772-1213. If you are hearing impaired call (800) 325-0778 TTY. You will need to give the Social Security Administration the full legal name of the decedent as well as his social security number and date of birth.

| *Special Situation* | DECEDENT RECEIVING SOCIAL SECURITY CHECKS |

If the decedent was receiving checks from Social Security, then you need to determine whether his last check needs to be returned to the Social Security Administration.

Each Social Security check is a payment for the prior month, provided that person lives for the entire prior month. If someone dies on the last day of the month, then you should not cash the check for that month. For example, if someone dies on July 31st, then you need to return the check that the agency mails out in August. If however, the decedent died on August 1st then the check sent in August need not be returned because that check is payment for the month of July.

If the Social Security check is electronically deposited into a bank account then notify the bank that the account holder died and notify the Social Security Administration as well. If the check needs to be returned, then the Social Security Administration will withdraw it electronically from the bank account. You will need to keep the account open until the funds are withdrawn.

 **SPOUSE**

SPOUSE/CHILD'S
SOCIAL SECURITY BENEFITS

If the decedent had sufficient work credits, the Social Security Administration will give the decedent's widow(er) or if unmarried, then the decedent's minor children, a one-time death benefit in the amount of $255.

SURVIVORS BENEFITS:

The spouse (or ex-spouse) of the decedent may be eligible for Survivors Benefits. Benefits vary depending on the amount of work credits earned by the decedent; whether the decedent had minor or disabled children; the spouse's age; how long they were married; etc.

The minor child of the decedent may be eligible for dependent child's benefits regardless of whether the decedent father ever married the child's mother. Paternity can be established by any one of several methods including the father acknowledging his child in writing or verbally to members of his family.

SOCIAL SECURITY BENEFITS

A spouse or ex-spouse can collect social security benefits based on the decedent's work record. This value may be greater than the spouse now receives. It is important to make an appointment with your local Social Security office and determine whether you as the spouse (or ex-spouse) or parent of decedent's minor child are eligible for any Social Security or Survivor benefit. The Social Security Administration has a web site from which you can down load publications that explain survivors benefits:

 SOCIAL SECURITY WEB SITE
http://www.ssa.gov

Special Situation	DECEDENT WITH GOVERNMENT PENSION

If the decedent was a federal retiree and received a government pension then any check received after the date of death needs to be returned to the U.S. Treasury. If the check is direct deposited to a bank account, then call the financial institution and ask them to return the check. If the check is sent by mail then you need to return it to: **Director, Regional Finance Center**
U. S. Treasury Department
P.O. Box 7367
Chicago, IL 60680
Include a letter explaining the reason for the return of the check and stating the decedent's date of death.

$$$ APPLY FOR BENEFITS $$$

Even though you notify the government of the death, they will not automatically give you benefits to which you may be entitled. You need to apply for those benefits by notifying the Office of Personnel Management ("OPM") of the death and requesting that they send you an application for survivor benefits. You can call them at **(888) 767-6738** or you can write to:
THE OFFICE OF PERSONNEL MANAGEMENT SERVICE
AND RECORDS CENTER
BOYERS, PA 16017

OPM WEB SITE
You can get assistance via E-mail at
retire@opm.gov
You will find brochures and information about
Survivor's Benefits at **http://www.opm.gov**

DECEDENT WITH COMPANY PENSION OR ANNUITY

In most cases, pension and annuity checks are payment for the prior month. If the decedent received his pension or annuity check before his death, then no monies need be returned. Pension checks and/or annuity checks received after the date of death may need to be returned to the company. You need to notify the company of the death to determine the status of the last check sent to the decedent.

Before notifying the company, locate the policy or pension statement that is the basis of the income. That document should tell whether there is a beneficiary of the pension or annuity funds now that the pensioner or annuitant is dead. If you cannot locate the document, use the return address on the check envelope and ask the company to send you a copy of the plan. Also request that they forward to you any claim form that may be required in order for the survivor or beneficiary to receive benefits under that pension plan or policy.

If the pension/annuity check is direct deposited to the decedent's account, then ask the bank to assist you in locating the company and notifying the company of the death.

| Special Situation | DECEDENT WITH AN IRA or a QUALIFIED RETIREMENT PLAN |

Anyone who is a beneficiary of an Individual Retirement Account ("IRA") or a Qualified Retirement Plan ("QRP") needs to keep in mind is that no income taxes have been paid on monies placed in an IRA or QRP account. Once monies are withdrawn, significant taxes may be due. You need to learn what options are available to you as a beneficiary of the plan and the tax consequences of each option. You will need to ask an accountant how much will be due in taxes for each option. Once you know all the facts, you will be able to make the best choice for your circumstance.

SPOUSE If the spouse is the beneficiary of the decedent's IRA account, then there are special options available. The spouse has the right to withdraw the money from the account or roll it over into the spouse's own retirement account. Although the employer can explain options that are available, the spouse still needs to understand the tax consequence of choosing any given option. It is important to consult with an accountant to determine the best way to go.

If the decedent had a QRP, the plan may permit the spouse to roll the balance of the account into a new IRA. The spouse needs to contact the decedent's employer for an explanation of the plan and all the options that are available at this time.

NOTIFYING IRS

THE FINAL INCOME TAX RETURN

The Personal Representative, or next of kin, needs to file the decedent's final federal income tax return (happily, there is no Texas state income tax). Filing the final return is done as part of filing the income tax return for the year of his death. If you have a joint bank account with the decedent, do not close that account until you determine whether the decedent is entitled to an income tax refund. See Chapter 6 for an explanation of how to obtain a refund from the IRS.

THE GOOD NEWS

Monies inherited from the decedent are not counted as income to you, so you do not pay federal income tax on those monies. If the monies you inherit later earn interest or income for you, then of course you will report that income as you do any other type of income.

Real and personal property inherited by a beneficiary is inherited at a "stepped up" basis. This means that if the decedent purchased some item that is now worth more than when he purchased it, then the beneficiary inherits the property at its fair market value as of the decedent's date of death. For example, suppose the decedent bought stock for $20,000 and it is now worth $50,000, then the beneficiary inherits the stock at the $50,000 value If the beneficiary sells the stock for $50,000, he pays no tax. If the beneficiary holds onto the stock and later sells it for $60,000, the beneficiary will pay federal capital gains tax only on the $10,000 increase in value since the decedent's death.

WHEN TO EVALUATE THE PROPERTY

The IRS gives you a choice of taking the value of the decedent's estate as of his date of death or 6 months later. For example, suppose the decedent's estate consists of stock worth $100,000 and you decide to hold onto them. If they increase in value so that 6 months later they are worth $110,000, you can (by filing the proper IRS tax return) to elect evaluate the decedent's estate at the six-month value in place of the date-of-death value. If you sell the stock at that time then you will not pay capital gains on the stock.

 If you hold onto the stock there is a risk that it will decrease in value during that six month period. If the stock goes down to $80,000, and you then sell, you only consolation will be that you can reflect the loss on your income tax statement.

Also, you need to consider the cost of employing an accountant (or a tax attorney) to file the necessary forms for the 6-month election. If you hold onto the stock and the increase in value is only a few thousand dollars, it may not pay to take the election. The cost in time and expense to make the election could be more than the tax payment itself.

 **SPOUSE**

WIDOW'S HOMESTEAD TAX BENEFITS

If the decedent had a homestead tax exemption because he was over 65, or because he was a disabled veteran, then that exemption may be transferable to his surviving spouse or minor child. If the exemption was because of age, then the exemption can be transferred to the spouse, provided the spouse is at least 55 years of age and continues to live in the home. If the surviving spouse is disabled and cannot work because of a physical or mental disability, then the spouse can also apply for a homestead disability exemption (Tax 11.13 (c), (q)). To apply for the exemption, the spouse will need to file an application with the local appraisal district office. You can find the telephone number and address in the telephone book or on the internet:

 TEXAS COMPTROLLER'S WEB SITE
http://www.window.state.tx.us/taxinfo/

CAPITAL GAINS EXCLUSION

In the tough "ole days" the IRS used to allow a once-in-a-lifetime, over age 55, up to $125,000 capital gains tax exclusion on the sale of the homestead. If a married couple sold their home and took the exclusion it was "used up" and no longer available to the other partner. In these, the good times, the IRS allows you to sell your homestead and up to $250,000 ($500,000 for a married couple) of the home-sale profit is tax free (IRC Section 121 B 3). There is no limit on the number of times you can use the exemption, provided you own and live in the homestead at least 2 years prior to the sale.

If the decedent and his spouse used their "once in a lifetime" homestead tax exemption, with this new law, the surviving spouse can sell the homestead and once again take advantage of a tax break.

An *estate tax* is a tax imposed by the federal and state government for the transfer of property at death. The *taxable estate* of the decedent is the total value of all of his property, as of his date of death. This includes real property (homestead, vacant lots, etc.) and personal property (cars, life insurance policies, business interests, securities, IRA accounts, etc.). It includes property held in the decedent's name alone, as well as property that he held jointly or in trust for another.

The Federal government gives each person an Estate and Gift Tax Exclusion amount. The state of Texas allows the same Exclusion value. No estate tax need be paid unless the decedent's taxable estate, plus gifts that he gave during his lifetime that exceeded $10,000 per person, per year, exceed the Exclusion amount. The Exclusion amount will increase each year until 2006:

YEAR	TAXABLE ESTATE
2000 — 2001	$675,000
2002 — 2003	$700,000
2004	$850,000
2005	$950,000
2006	$1,000,000

No Texas Inheritance Tax Return or Federal Estate tax return need be filed unless the decedent's taxable estate and lifetime gifts exceed the scheduled amount as of his date of death. If the amount is exceeded, then an Estate tax return (IRS form 706) and a Texas Inheritance tax return (Comptroller Form 17-106) must be filed. There is an unlimited marital tax deduction, so if the decedent was married, no estate tax need be paid; however if the decedent's taxable estate exceeds the stated value, an estate tax return still must be filed.

DECEDENT WITH A TRUST

If the decedent was the Grantor (or Settlor) of a trust, then he was probably managing the trust as Trustee during his lifetime. The trust document should name a *Successor Trustee* to manage the trust now that the Grantor is deceased. The trust document may instruct the Successor Trustee to make certain gifts once the Grantor dies or the trust document may direct the Successor Trustee to hold money in trust for a beneficiary of the trust.

☎ **LAWYER**

IF YOU ARE SUCCESSOR TRUSTEE

If you are the Successor Trustee then in addition to following the terms of the trust, you are required to obey all of the laws of the state of Texas relating to the administration of the trust. You should consult with an attorney experienced in Estate Planning to explain to you how to properly administer the trust and to ensure that you do so without any liability to yourself.

IF YOU ARE A BENEFICIARY

If you are a beneficiary of the trust, then you need to obtain a copy of the trust and see how the trust is to be administered now that the Grantor or Settlor is deceased. Most trust documents are written in "legalese," so you may want to employ your own attorney to review the trust, and explain what rights you have under that trust. If you cannot afford an attorney, then you can at least, make a written demand for a full accounting. The Trustee is required by law to give you this information (Property 113.151).

NOTIFYING THE BUSINESS COMMUNITY

People and companies who were doing business with the decedent need to be notified of his death. This includes utility companies, credit card companies, banks, brokerage firms and any company that insured the decedent.

NOTIFY CREDIT CARD COMPANIES

You need to notify the decedent's credit card companies of the death. If you can find the contract with the credit card company check to see whether the decedent had credit card insurance. If the decedent had credit card insurance, then the balance of the account is now paid in full. If you cannot find the contract, then contact the company and get a copy of the contract along with a statement of the balance due as of the date of death.

DESTROY DECEDENT'S CREDIT CARDS

You should destroy all of the decedent's credit cards. If you hold a credit card jointly with the decedent, then it is important to waste no time in closing that account and opening another in your name only.

That's something Barbara knows from hard experience. She and Hank never married but they did live together for several years before he died from liver disease. Hank came from a well to do family so he had enough money to support himself and Barbara during his long illness. Hank put Barbara on all of his credit card accounts so that she could purchase things when he became too ill to go shopping with her. After the funeral, Barbara had a gathering of friends and family at their apartment. Barbara was so preoccupied with her loss that she never noticed that Hank's credit cards were missing until the bills started coming in.

Barbara did not know who ran up the bills on Hank's credit cards during the month following his death. It was obvious that Hank's signature had been forged — but who forged it? One credit card company suspected that it might have been Barbara herself. Because the cards were held jointly, Barbara became liable to either pay the debts or prove that she did not make the purchases. She was able to clear her credit record but it took several months and she had to employ an attorney to do so.

NOTIFY INSURANCE COMPANIES

Examine the decedent's financial records to determine the name and telephone number of all of the companies that insured the decedent or his property. This includes real property insurance, motor vehicle insurance, health insurance and life insurance.

MOTOR VEHICLE INSURANCE

If the decedent owned any type of motor vehicle (car, truck, boat, airplane) locate the insurance policy on that vehicle and notify the insurance company of the death. Determine how long insurance coverage continues after the death. Ask the insurance agent to explain what things are covered under the policy. Is the motor vehicle covered for all types of casualty (theft, accident, vandalism, etc.) or is coverage limited in some way?

If you can continue coverage then determine when the next insurance payment is due. Hopefully, the car will be sold or transferred to a beneficiary before that date, but if not, then you need to arrange to continue with insurance coverage.

┌───┐
│ **Special** 〉 ACCIDENTAL DEATH
│ **Situation**

Special Situation ACCIDENTAL DEATH

If the decedent died as a result of an accident, then check for all possible sources of accident insurance coverage including his homeowner's policy. Some credit card companies provide free accident insurance as part of their contract with their card holders.

If the decedent died in an automobile accident, check to see whether he was covered by any type of travel insurance, such as rental car insurance. If he belonged to an automobile club, such as AAA, then check whether he had accident insurance as part of his club membership.

LIFE INSURANCE

If the decedent had life insurance, then you need to locate the policy and notify the company of his death. Call each life insurance company and ask what they require in order to forward the insurance proceeds to the beneficiary. Most companies will ask you to send them the original policy and a certified copy of the death certificate.

Send the original policy by certified mail or any of the overnight services that require a signed receipt for the package. Make a copy of the original policy for your records before mailing the original policy to the company.

IF YOU CANNOT LOCATE THE POLICY

If you know that the decedent was insured but you cannot locate the insurance policy, the AMERICAN COUNCIL OF LIFE INSURANCE ("ACLI") may be able to help you. Write to the ACLI giving them the name, address, date of birth, and social security number of the decedent. Their address is:

POLICY SEARCH ACLI
1000 Pennsylvania Avenue, NW
Washington, DC 20004

The ACLI will assist you by asking the 100 largest insurance companies in the nation to search their records for the missing policy. If it is found, you will receive a copy of the policy free of charge.

IF YOU CANNOT LOCATE THE COMPANY

If you cannot locate the insurance company it may be doing business under another name or it may no longer be doing business in the state of Texas. Each state has a branch of government that regulates insurance companies doing business in that state. If you are having difficulty locating the insurance company call the Department of Insurance in the state where the policy was purchased and ask for assistance in locating the company. The number for the Texas Department of Insurance is (800) 252-3439.

 EAGLE PUBLISHING COMPANY WEB SITE gives the telephone number of the Department of Insurance for each state: http://www.eaglepublishing.com

WORK RELATED INSURANCE

If the decedent was employed then his employer may provide survivor benefits from a company or group life insurance plan and/or a retirement plan. If the decedent belonged to a union, then check with the union to determine whether members of the union receive any death benefits.

The decedent may have belonged to a professional, fraternal or social organization such as the local Chamber of Commerce, a Veteran's organization, the Kiwanis, AARP, the Rotary Club, etc. If he belonged to any such organization check to see whether the organization provided any type of insurance coverage.

Special Situation ➤ **BUSINESS OWNED BY DECEDENT**

If the decedent owned his own company he may have purchased "key man" insurance. Key man insurance is a policy designed to protect the company should a valuable employee become disabled or die. Benefits are paid to the company to compensate the company for the loss of someone who is essential to the continuation of the business. Ultimately the policy benefits those who inherit the business.

If the decedent owned shares in the company or was a partner in the company, there may be a shareholder's agreement or partnership agreement that requires the company to use the insurance proceeds to purchase the shares or buy out the partnership interest owned by the decedent. If there is a probate procedure, then the Personal Representative's attorney will need to review the agreement. If the decedent died without a Will, then the next of kin needs to find out what rights (if any) the family has in the business or to the proceeds of the key man insurance policy.

Special Situation	CORPORATE OWNER OR RESIDENT AGENT

If the decedent was the sole owner and officer of a corporation then the Texas Secretary of State needs to be notified of the change. There will need to be a probate procedure to determine the new owner of the company so it may take some period of time before new officers and directors are identified. The law requires each corporation to maintain a registered office and a resident agent at that address (Business Corp. 2.09, 2.10).

If the decedent was the resident agent of a corporation, then a new resident agent needs to be appointed as soon as is practicable. Forms to change officers, directors and registered agents can be obtained by calling the Corporations Section of the Secretary of State: (800) 252-1386 or by writing to them at:
                P.O. Box 13697, Austin, TX 78711
or you can download the forms from their Web site:

 TEXAS SECRETARY OF STATE WEB SITE
http://www.sos.state.tx.us/function/forms/formidx.html

If you were not actively involved in running the business, then you might request a status report of the company. The report will show whether filing fees are current and will identify the officers and directors of the company. The Texas Comptroller of Public Accounts has a Web Site from which you can print a Certificate of Account Status letter and get information about the officers and directors of the corporation:

 COMPTROLLERS OF PUBLIC ACCOUNTS WEB SITE
            http://open.cpa.state.tx.us/

HOMEOWNER'S INSURANCE

If the decedent owned his own home, then check whether there is sufficient insurance coverage on the property. The decedent may have neglected to increase his insurance as the property appreciated in value. If you think the property may be vacant for some period of time, then it is important to have vandalism coverage included in the policy. Once the property is sold, or transferred to the proper beneficiary, you can have the policy discontinued or transferred to the new owner. The decedent's estate should receive a rebate for the unused portion of the premium.

NOTIFY THE HOMEOWNER'S ASSOCIATION

If the decedent owned a condominium or a residence regulated by a homeowner's association, then the association needs to be notified of the death. Once the property is transferred to the proper beneficiary, he/she will need to contact the association and arrange to have notices of dues or assessments forwarded to the new owner.

MORTGAGE INSURANCE

If the decedent had a mortgage on any parcel of real estate that he owned, he might have arranged with his lender for an insurance policy that pays off the mortgage balance in the event of his death. Look at the closing statement to see if there was a charge for mortgage insurance. Also, check with the lender to determine if such a policy was purchased.

If the decedent was the sole owner of the property, then the beneficiary of that property needs to make arrangements to continue payment of the mortgage until title to the property is transferred to that beneficiary.

HEALTH INSURANCE

If the decedent was covered by health insurance, then the insurance carrier probably knows of the death, but it is a good idea to contact them to determine what coverage the decedent had under that insurance plan. If you cannot find the original policy, have the insurance company send you a copy of the policy so that you can determine whether medical treatment given to the decedent before his death was covered by that policy.

DECEDENT ON MEDICARE

If the decedent was covered by Medicare, you do not need to notify anyone, but you do need to know what things were covered by Medicare so that you can determine what medical bills are (or are not) covered by Medicare. The publication MEDICARE AND YOU explains what things are covered. The book is available in regular print (Publication HCFA 10050) and in large print (Publication HCFA 10050-LE). You can get the book by writing to:

U.S. GOVERNMENT PRINTING OFFICE
U.S. Dept. of Health and Human Services
Health Care Financing Administration
7500 Security Boulevard
Baltimore, MD 21244-1850

You can also find the publication on the Internet:

 MEDICARE WEB SITE
http:/www.medicare.gov

If you have questions about Medicare coverage, there is a toll-free Medicare Hotline (800)633-4227. English and Spanish speaking operators are available Monday through Friday from 8 a.m. to 4:30 p.m. For the hearing impaired call TTY/TDD (877) 486-2048.

THE SPOUSE'S HEALTH INSURANCE

If the spouse of the decedent is insured under Medicare, then the death does not affect the surviving spouse's coverage. If spouse was not covered by Medicare but has her own health insurance that also covered the decedent, then the spouse needs to notify the employer of the death because this may affect the cost of the plan to the employer and/or the spouse.

If the spouse was covered under the decedent's policy then he/she needs to arrange for new coverage. There are state and federal laws that ensure continued coverage under the decedent's policy for a period of time depending on whether the decedent's employer falls under federal or state regulation.

If the decedent was employed by a federally regulated company (usually a company with at least twenty employees) then under the Consolidated Omnibus Budget Reconciliation Act ("COBRA") the employer must make the company health plan available to the surviving spouse and any dependent child of the decedent for at least 36 months. The employer is required to give notice to the surviving spouse that the spouse and/or dependent child have the right to continue coverage under the decedent's health plan. The spouse and/or child have 60 days from the date of death or 60 days after the employer sends notice (whichever is later) to tell the employer whether the surviving spouse and child wish to continue with the health insurance plan.

SPOUSE'S HEALTH INSURANCE (continued)

The only problem with continued coverage may be the cost. Before the death, the employer may have been paying some percentage of the premium. The employer has no such duty after the death unless there was some employment agreement stating otherwise. Under COBRA, the employer may charge the spouse for the full cost of the plan plus a 2% administrative fee.

You can find additional information about COBRA in the publication **PENSION AND HEALTH CARE COVERAGE**. This and other publications can be found at the U.S. Department of Labor Web site:

 DEPARTMENT OF LABOR WEB SITE
http://www.dol.gov/dol/pwba

HEALTH INSURANCE UNDER TEXAS LAW

If the decedent's employer is not regulated under COBRA, and the spouse is unable to continue coverage under the decedent's plan, then the spouse may be eligible for coverage under the Health Insurance Risk Pool. The Pool was created to cover those people who cannot obtain coverage because of a pre-existing condition. It is also eligible to those who cannot obtain health insurance except at a rate that is higher than the Pool rate. To obtain information about applying for insurance under the Health Insurance Risk Pool call (888) 398-3927, or check out their Web site:

 HEALTH INSURANCE RISK POOL
http://www.txhealthpool.com

✍ CHANGE BENEFICIARY ✍

If the decedent was someone you named as beneficiary of your insurance policy, Will or trust, brokerage account or pension plan, then you may need to name another beneficiary in his place:

INSURANCE POLICY ✍
If you named the decedent as the primary beneficiary of your life insurance policy, then check to see whether you named a contingent (alternate) beneficiary in the event that the decedent did not survive you. If not, then you need to contact the insurance company and name a new beneficiary. If you did name a contingent beneficiary, then that person is now your primary beneficiary and you need to consider whether you wish to name a new contingent beneficiary at this time.

HEALTH INSURANCE POLICY ✍
If the decedent was covered under your health insurance policy, then your employer and the health insurer need to be notified of the death because this may affect the cost of the plan to you and/or your employer.

WILL OR TRUST ✍
Most Wills provide for a contingent beneficiary in the event that the person named as beneficiary dies first. If you named the decedent as your beneficiary, then check to see whether you named an alternate beneficiary. If not, you need to have your attorney revise your Will and name a new beneficiary.

Similarly, if you are the Grantor or Settlor of a trust and the decedent was one of the beneficiaries of your trust, then check the trust document to see if you named an alternate beneficiary. If not, contact your attorney to prepare an amendment to the trust, naming a new beneficiary.

BANK AND SECURITIES ACCOUNTS ✍

If the decedent was a beneficiary of your bank or securities account, or if the decedent was a joint owner of your bank account or securities account, then it is important to contact the financial institution and tell them about the death. You may wish to arrange for a new beneficiary or joint owner at this time.

PENSION PLANS ✍

If the decedent was a beneficiary under your pension plan, then you need to notify them of his death and name a new beneficiary. Many pension plans require that you notify them within a set period of time (usually 30 days) so it is important to notify them as soon as you are able. If the decedent was a beneficiary of your Individual Retirement Account ("IRA") or of your Qualified Retirement Plan ("QRP") and you did not provide for an alternate beneficiary, then you need to name someone at this time.

There are many government regulations relating to IRA and QRP accounts. For example, you must begin to withdraw money from the account on April 1st of the year after you reach the age of 70 1/2. How much you must withdraw depends on whether you choose to base the amount withdrawn on your own life expectancy or on the joint life expectancy of you and your oldest beneficiary. If you have not reached the age of 70 1/2, then before naming a new beneficiary, you may wish to consult with your accountant or estate planning attorney to decide which is the best option for you.

NOTIFYING CREDITORS

If the decedent owed money, and a probate procedure is necessary, then it will be the job of the person who is appointed as Personal Representative to give written notice of the death to all of the decedent's creditors. The attorney who handles the probate will explain to the Personal Representative how notice is to be given.

If no probate procedure is necessary, then the next of kin can notify the creditors of the death, but before doing so, first read Chapter 4: WHAT BILLS NEED TO BE PAID? That chapter explains what bills need to be paid and who is responsible to pay them, but before any bill can be paid, you need to know what the decedent owned as of his date of death. The next chapter explains how to identify, and then locate all of the property owned by the decedent.

Locating the Assets   3

It is important to locate the financial records of the decedent and then carefully examine those records. Even the partner of a long-term marriage should conduct a thorough search because the surviving spouse may be unaware of all that was owned (or owed) by the decedent.

It is not unusual for a surviving spouse to be surprised when learning of the decedent's business transactions — especially in those cases where the decedent had control of family finances. One such example is that of Sam and Henrietta. They married just as soon as Sam was discharged from the army after World War II. During their marriage, Sam handled all of the finances giving Henrietta just enough money to run the household.

Every now and again Henrietta would think of getting a job. She longed to have her own source of income and some economic independence. Each time she brought up the subject Sam would loudly object. He had no patience for this new "woman's lib" thing. Sam said he got married to have a real wife — one who would cook his meals and keep house for him.

Henrietta was not the arguing type. She rationalized, saying that Sam had a delicate stomach and dust allergies. He needed her to prepare his special meals and keep an immaculate house for him. Besides, Sam had a good job with a major cruise line and he needed her to accompany him on his frequent business trips.

Once Sam retired, he was even more cautious in his spending habits. Henrietta seldom complained. She assumed the reason for his "thrift" was that they had little money and had to live on his pension.

They were married 52 years when Sam died at the age of 83. Henrietta was 81 at the time of his death. She was one very happy, very angry and very aged widow when she discovered that Sam left her with assets worth well over a million dollars!

LOCATING FINANCIAL RECORDS

To locate the decedent's assets you need to find evidence of what he owned and where those assets are located. His financial records should lead you to the location of all of his assets so your first job is to locate those records. The best place to start the search is in the decedent's home. Many people keep their financial records in a single place but it is important to check the entire house to be sure you did not miss something.

CHECK THE COMPUTER

Don't overlook that computer sitting silently in the corner. It may hold the decedent's check register and all of the decedent's financial records. The computer may be programmed to protect information. If you cannot access the decedent's records, you may need to employ a computer technician or computer consultant who will be able to print out all of the information on the hard drive of the computer. You can find such a technician or consultant by looking in the telephone book under
COMPUTER SUPPORT SERVICES   or
COMPUTER SYSTEM DESIGNS & CONSULTANTS.

COLLECT AND IDENTIFY KEYS

The decedent may have kept his records in a safe deposit box, so you may find that your first job is to locate the keys to the box. As you go through the personal effects of the decedent, collect and identify all the keys that you find. If you come across an unidentified key, it could be a key to a post office box (private or federal) or a safe deposit box located in a bank or in a private vault company. You will need to determine whether that key opens a box that contains property belonging to the decedent or whether the key is to a box no longer in use. Some ways to investigate are as follows:

☑ CHECK BUSINESS RECORDS

If the decedent kept receipts, look through those items to see if he paid for the rental of a post office or safe deposit box. Also, check his check register to see if he wrote out a check to the Postmaster or to any safe deposit or vault company. Look at his bank statements to see if there is any bank charge for a safe deposit box. Some banks bill separately for safe deposit boxes so check with all of the banks in which the decedent had an account to determine if he had a box with that bank.

☑ CHECK THE KEY TYPE

If you cannot identify the key take the key to all of the local locksmiths and ask whether anyone can identify the type of facility that uses such keys. If that doesn't work then go to each bank, post office and private safe deposit boxes located in places where the decedent shopped, worked or frequented and ask whether they use the type of key that you found.

☑ CHECK THE MAIL

Check the mail over the next several months to see if the decedent receives a statement requesting payment for the next year's rental of a post office or safe deposit box.

You may find evidence of a brokerage account, bank account, or safe deposit box by examining correspondence addressed to the decedent. If the decedent was living alone, then have the mail forwarded to the person he named as Personal Representative or Executor of his Will. If the decedent did not leave a Will then the mail should be forwarded to his next of kin. Call the Postmaster and ask him/her to send you the necessary forms to make the change. Request that the mail be forwarded for the longest period allowed by law (currently one year).

The decedent may have been renting a post office box at his local post office branch or perhaps at the branch closest to where he did his banking. Ask the Postmaster to help you determine whether the decedent was renting a post office box. If so, then you need to locate the key to the box so that you can collect the decedent's mail.

Special Situation ▷ **LOST POST OFFICE BOX KEY**

If the decedent had a post office box and you cannot locate the key, then contact the local postmaster and ask him/her what documentation is needed for you to gain possession of the mail in that box. As before, you will ask the Postmaster to have all future mail addressed to that box, forwarded to the Personal Representative, or if there is no Will, then to the decedent's next of kin.

WHAT TO DO WITH CHECKS

You may receive checks in the mail made out to the decedent. Social security checks, pension checks and annuity checks issued after the date of death may need to be returned to the sender. (See pages 28 and 30 of this book.) Other checks need to be deposited to the decedent's bank account. The decedent is not here to endorse the check, but you can deposit to his account by writing his bank account number on the back of the check and printing beneath it "FOR DEPOSIT ONLY."

The bank will accept such an endorsement and deposit the check into the decedent's account. If the check is significant in value and/or the decedent had different accounts that are accessible to different people, then there needs to be cooperation and a sense of fair play. If not, the dollar gain may not nearly offset the emotional turmoil. Such was the case with Gail. Her father made her a joint owner of his checking account to assist in paying his bills. He had macular degeneration and it was increasingly difficult for him to see. The father also had a savings account that was in his name only.

Gail's brother, Ken, had a good paying job in Canada. Even though he lived at a distance, Ken, his wife and two children always spent Christmas with his father. Gail's good cooking added to the festivities. Each summer, their father enjoyed leaving the heat of Texas to spend a few weeks with Richard in the cool Canadian climate.

One July, the father purchased a round trip ticket to Canada. It cost several hundred dollars. Just before the departure date, the father had a heart attack and died. Gail called the airline to cancel the ticket. They refunded the money in a check made out to her father. She deposited the check to the joint account.

As part of the probate procedure, the money in the father's savings account was divided equally between Ken and his sister. Ken wondered what happened to the money from the airline tickets.

Gail explained "He paid for the tickets from the joint account, so I deposited the money back to that account. "

"Aren't you going to give me half?"

"Dad meant for me to have whatever was in that joint account. If he wanted you to have half of the money, he would have made you joint owner as well."

Ken didn't see it that way: "That refund was part of Dad's probate estate. It should have been deposited to his savings account to be divided equally between us. Are you going force me to argue this in court?"

Gail finally agreed to split the money with Ken, but the damage was done. Gail complains that holidays are lonely since her father died.

COLLECTING LEGAL DOCUMENTS

As you go through the papers of the decedent you may come across documents that indicate property ownership, such as bank registers, stock or bond certificates, insurance policies, brokerage account statements, etc. You will need these documents in order to transfer title to the proper beneficiary.

COLLECT CERTIFICATE OF TITLE TO MOTOR VEHICLE
You will need the decedent's certificate of title in order to transfer the decedent's mtor vehicle. Chapter 6 explains how to transfer the property to the proper beneficiary. If you are unable to locate the certificate of title, then turn to that chapter for information about how to obtain a copy.

COLLECT DEEDS
Collect the deeds to all property owned by the decedent. Many people keep deeds in a safe deposit box. If you cannot find the deed in the decedent's home, then you need to determine whether he had a safe deposit box. If you know that the decedent owned real property (lot, residence, condominium, cooperative, time share, etc.) but you cannot locate the deed, then contact the Clerk in the records division of the county where the property is located. The Clerk can provide you with a certified copy of the last recorded deed.

You will need to identify the parcel of land by giving the legal description of the land or its parcel identification number. You can find this information on the last tax bill sent to the decedent. If you cannot find the last property tax bill, then call the county property appraiser's office and they will give you the information. You can use the same procedure if you cannot locate the deed to property owned by the decedent in another state, namely, check with the recording department in the county where the property is located.

Special Situation > DECEDENT'S RESIDENTIAL LEASE

If the decedent was renting his residence, then he may have a written lease agreement. It is important to locate the lease because the decedent's estate may be responsible for payments under the lease. If you cannot locate the lease, then ask the landlord for a copy. If the landlord reports that there was no written lease, then verify that the decedent was on a month to month basis and then work out a mutually agreeable time in which to vacate the premises.

If a written lease is in effect, then determine the end of the lease period. If that date is more than a couple of months away, then ask the landlord whether he will agree to cancel the lease on the condition that the property is left in good condition. If the landlord wants to hold the estate liable for the balance of the lease, then it is prudent to have an attorney review the lease to determine what rights and responsibilities remain now that the tenant is deceased.

 LAWYER | DECEDENT'S ONGOING BUSINESS

If the decedent had his own business or was a partner or shareholder of a small company, then the Personal Representative (or next of kin, if no probate is necessary) needs to contact the company accountant to obtain the company's business records. If there is a company attorney, then contact him/her for assistance in continuing to operate the business or terminating it. If you are a beneficiary of the estate, consider consulting with your own attorney to determine your rights and responsibilities in the business.

COLLECT TAX RECORDS

You will need to file the decedent's final state and federal income tax return so you need to collect all of his tax records that he filed for the past 3 years. If you cannot locate his prior tax records, then check his personal telephone book and/or his personal bank register to see if he employed an accountant. If you can locate his accountant, then contact the accountant to see if he/she has a copy of those records.

If you are unable to locate the decedent's federal tax records then they can be obtained from the IRS. The IRS will send copies of the decedent's tax filings to anyone who has a *fiduciary relationship* with the decedent. The IRS considers the following people to be fiduciaries:

➢ the person named as Executor in the decedent's Will

➢ the person appointed as the Personal Representative of the decedent's estate

➢ the successor trustee of the decedent's trust

➢ if the person died intestate, then whoever is legally entitled to possession of the decedent's property (See Chapter 5 to learn who are the beneficiaries.)

The fiduciary can receive copies of the decedent's tax filings by notifying IRS that he/she is acting in a fiduciary capacity, and then requesting the copies.

To notify the IRS of the fiduciary capacity file Form 56:
 NOTICE CONCERNING FIDUCIARY RELATIONSHIP

To request the copies, file IRS Form 4506:
 REQUEST FOR COPY OR TRANSCRIPT OF TAX FORM

Your accountant can file these forms for you or you can obtain the forms from the IRS by calling (800) 829-3676. These forms can be downloaded from the Internet:

IRS FORMS WEB SITE
http://www.irs.gov./forms_pubs/forms.html

LOCATE OUT OF STATE ACCOUNTS

If the decedent had out of state bank or brokerage accounts, then you might be able to locate them if they mail the decedent monthly or quarterly statements. Not all institutions do so, but all institutions are required to send out an IRS tax form 1099 each year giving the amount of interest earned on that account. Once those forms come in, you will learn the location of all of the decedent's active accounts.

FINDING LOST/ ABANDONED PROPERTY

If the decedent was forgetful, he may have money in a lost bank or securities account or abandoned safe deposit box. Texas law requires that if an account has been inactive for a period of time and the location of the owner of the property cannot be determined after a diligent search, then the property is turned over to the Texas Comptroller.
The period of time varies:

- ⌛ 3 years for a check
- ⌛ 5 years for a checking or savings account
- ⌛ 5 years for a safe deposit box
- ⌛ 5 years for a money order
- ⌛ 15 years for a traveler's check

(Property Chap. 72 & 73)

The state will try to locate the owner. They regularly publish a list of owner's names in major newspapers throughout Texas. If the state cannot locate the owner, they will sell the property. If the owner, or the decedent owner's heir, later requests the property, then the state will give them the proceeds of the sale.

You can determine whether there is a record identifying the decedent as the owner of abandoned property by calling the Comptroller's office at (800) 321-2274, or by writing to: TEXAS COMPTROLLER OF PUBLIC ACCOUNTS
UNCLAIMED PROPERTY SECTION
P.O. Box 12019
Austin, TX 78711-2019

The Comptroller's office has a Web site where you can obtain information about unclaimed property:

 **TEXAS COMPTROLLER OF PUBLIC ACCOUNTS
UNCLAIMED PROPERTY**
http:// www.cpa.state.tx.us/comptrol/unclprop/
E-mail: unclaimed.property@cpa.state.tx.us

To make a claim for the property, you will need to give the full legal name of the decedent, his social security number and all previous Texas addresses.

CLAIMS IN OTHER STATES

Each state has an agency or department that is responsible for handling lost, abandoned or unclaimed property located within that state. If the decedent had residences in other states, then call the UNCLAIMED or ABANDONED PROPERTY department to see if the decedent has unclaimed property in that state.

 EAGLE PUBLISHING COMPANY OF BOCA
lists telephone numbers for the
unclaimed property division for
each state at their web site:
http://www.eaglepublishing.com

CLAIMS FOR DECEDENT VICTIMS OF HOLOCAUST
The New York State Banking Department has a special Claims Processing Office for Holocaust survivors or their heirs. The office processes claims for Swiss bank accounts that were dormant since the end of World War II. You can call them at (800) 695-3318.

LOCATE CONTRACTS

If the decedent belonged to a health club or gym, he may have prepaid for the year. Look for the club contract. It will give the terms of the agreement. If you cannot locate the contract then contact the company for a copy of the agreement. If the contract was prepaid, then determine whether the agreement provides for a refund for the unused portion.

SERVICE CONTRACT

Many people purchase appliance service contracts to have their appliances serviced in the event that an appliance should need repair. If the decedent had a security system then he may have had a service contract with a company to monitor the system and contact the police in the event of a break-in.

If the decedent had a service contract, then you need to locate it and determine whether it can be assigned to the new owner of the property. If the contract is assignable, the new owner can reimburse the decedent's estate for the unused portion. If the contract cannot be assigned, then once the property is transferred, try to obtain a refund for the unused portion of the contract.

LOCATING THE WILL

If you have the decedent's Will in your possession, then as soon as you receive notice of the death, you are required, by law, to deliver it to the Clerk of the Probate division of the County courthouse in the county where the decedent lived. If the decedent did not live in Texas, but he had property here, then you can deposit the Will in the county where the property is located. If he had property in several locations and he died in Texas, then you can deposit the Will in the county where he died (Probate Chap. I, Sec. 6(b) and Chap V, Sec. 75)

Call the Clerk and ask for directions to the Probate division of the County Court. The Clerk will accept an original Will only and not a copy, so it is important to hand carry the original document to the Clerk. If you are unable to make the delivery in person, you may mail the Will to the Clerk, but send it by certified mail so that you will have proof of delivery. Make a copy of the Will for your own records before delivering it to the court. Once the Will is deposited with the court, the Clerk keeps it until someone begins a probate procedure. It may be that no probate procedure is necessary, in which case the Will remains in possession of the Probate court.

DECEDENT WITH OUT OF STATE RESIDENCE

If the decedent had his principal residence in another state, then before you deposit the Will, consult with an attorney experienced in Probate matters to determine whether the Will needs to be probated in Texas or in the state of his residence. If the Will is to be probated in another state, then it is best to contact an attorney in that state and arrange to have the Will deposited with the Probate court in the state of his residence.

THE MISSING WILL

It has been estimated that 70% of the population do not have a Will, so if you cannot find a Will, chances are that the decedent did not have one. If you suspect that the decedent had a Will, but you cannot find it, then there are at least three places to check out:

⇨ **THE CLERK OF THE COUNTY COURT**

Texas law gives residents the right to deposit their Will with the County Clerk in the county of their residence. At the time of deposit the decedent will tell the Clerk who is to be given the Will once he dies. The Clerk will give the maker of the Will a Certificate of Deposit as evidence of the receipt the Will.

If the decedent's Will is deposited with the Clerk, then the Clerk will give the Will to the person requested by the decedent. If you are that person, then all you need do to get the Will is to give the Clerk the Certificate of Deposit.

If you cannot find a Certificate of Deposit, then contact the Clerk and ask whether a Will is on deposit with the court. If the Will is in the court, then you can get it by signing an *affidavit* (a sworn written statement) stating that the Certificate of Deposit is either lost, stolen or destroyed (Probate Chap IV, Sec. 71).

⇨ **THE SAFE DEPOSIT BOX**

If you believe that the decedent had a Will but you cannot find it, then check to see if the decedent had a safe deposit box. If he did, you will need to gain entry to that box to see whether the Will is in the box. See page 69 for an explanation of how to gain entry to the safe deposit box.

⇨ THE DECEDENT'S ATTORNEY

Look at the decedent's checkbook for the past few years and see whether he paid any attorney fees. If you are able to locate the decedent's attorney, then call and inquire whether the attorney ever drafted a Will for the decedent, and if so, whether the attorney has the original Will in his possession. If the attorney has the original Will, then ask the attorney to forward the Will to the probate court. Asking the attorney to forward the Will to the court does not obligate you to employ the attorney should you later find that a probate procedure is necessary.

 **LAWYER**   A COPY BUT NO ORIGINAL

If you have a copy of the Will but cannot locate the original then the Probate court might allow the estate of the decedent to be probated using the copy, provided you can prove that the document is a true copy of the decedent's valid, unrevoked Will (Probate Chap.V, Sec. 85). You will need to employ an attorney who is experienced in probate matters to present such proof to the court.

```
┌─────────────────────────────────────────────────┐
│  ┌──────────────┐                                 │
│  │ Special      ╲    WILL DRAFTED IN ANOTHER      │
│  │ Situation    ╱      STATE OR COUNTRY           │
│  └──────────────┘                                 │
```

If a Will is drafted in another state or country, then it can be submitted to the County Clerk for probate in the state of Texas. If the decedent was a resident of Texas, then the Will must be proved to be valid in the same manner as any other Will admitted to probate (see Chapter 8 for an explanation of what makes a valid Will). If the Will is written in a foreign language, then it will need to be accompanied by a true and complete English translation before it can be admitted to Probate.

Sometimes it happens that the decedent is a resident of another state, but he has property in Texas. If there needs to be a probate procedure in the state of Texas in addition to a probate procedure in the state of his residence, then a certified copy of the Will his out-of-state Will needs to be submitted to the County Clerk in the county where the decedent's Texas property is located. If the Will has been admitted to probate in the state of his residence, then his Will is acceptable in Texas, regardless of whether that Will is drafted in conformity with Texas law (Probate, Chap. V, Sec. 95(a), (e)).

ACCESSING THE SAFE DEPOSIT BOX

If the decedent had a safe deposit box and he was the only person with access to the safe deposit box, then Texas Statute requires that the bank (or safe deposit box lessor) allow any of the following people to examine the contents of the box:

- ▷ the decedent's spouse
- ▷ a parent of the decedent
- ▷ an adult child or grandchild of the decedent
- ▷ the person named as Executor in a copy of the decedent's Will

This statute requires that a company officer be present when the safe deposit box is opened (Probate Chap. 1, Sec. 36 (D)). If you are any of the above persons and you need to get into the safe deposit box, then call the bank ahead of time and make an appointment to meet with an officer of the company.

If you are gaining access because you are named as the Executor of the Will, then you need to bring a copy of the Will with you. Ask the bank what other identification they will require of you. Most companies require that you bring a certified copy of the death certificate, so you may need to wait until you receive the death certificate to prove to the bank officials that the owner of the box is dead.

THE CONTENTS OF THE BOX

If the original Will is found in the box, then upon your request the bank will deliver the Will to the Clerk of the County Court of the county where the decedent resided, or they can give it to the person named as Executor of the Will. If they give it to the Executor, then the bank is required to make a copy of the Will and to keep it for four years after the date of delivery.

If there is a deed to the decedent's burial plot in the safe deposit box, then the bank can give that deed to you. Also, if there is a life insurance policy in the safe deposit box then the bank has the authority to give the policy to the beneficiary named in the policy. Nothing else may be removed from the safe deposit box without an order from the Probate court (Probate Chap. 1, Sec. 36(E)).

If you find other valuables in the box that need to be removed from the box, then you need to go through some kind of probate procedure to get possession of those items. Ask the officer of the company to make an inventory of the contents of the decedent's safe deposit box using the company letterhead.

See Chapter 6 for an explanation of what type of probate procedure may be necessary in your case in order to get possession of the contents of the safe deposit box.

What Bills Need To Be Paid? 4

If the estate of the decedent has sufficient assets, then the Personal Representative of the decedent's estate has the duty to be sure that all of the decedent's valid bills are paid. If the decedent had many debts, but no money or property, then of course, there is no way to pay the bills. The only remaining question is whether anyone else is responsible to pay those bills. If the decedent was married, then the first person the creditor will look to, is the decedent's spouse. To understand the basis of this expectation, you need to know a bit of the history of our legal system.

Under English Common law, a husband was legally held responsible for his wife's debts because, once a woman married, her legal identity merged with that of her husband. A married woman had no right to own property or to enter into a contract in her own name. Once married, a woman became totally dependent on her husband and he was legally responsible to provide her with basic necessities — food, clothing, shelter and medical services. If anyone provided these necessities to his wife, then, regardless of whether the husband agreed to be responsible for the debt, he became obliged to pay for them. This law was called the DOCTRINE OF NECESSARIES.

The United States inherited its legal system from England, but over the years each state developed its own set of laws relating to spousal responsibility. Some states decided to make the Doctrine of Necessaries part of their state law. Other states, such as New Jersey, decided to apply the Doctrine equally to both sexes, making the husband responsible to pay for his wife's necessaries and the wife responsible to pay for her husband's necessaries. Other states, such as Florida, abolished the law altogether. In these states neither spouse is liable for the debts of the other unless the spouse agrees to pay the debt.

Texas is a Community Property state. Whether the spouse is liable to pay the decedent's debts depends on whether the property owned by the surviving spouse is separate property or community property. Texas statute (Family 3.001) defines *Separate property* as:

⇉ property owned by the spouse prior to the marriage
⇉ property received as a gift or an inheritance during the marriage
⇉ monies received as a result of personal injuries during the marriage, not including any money for loss of earnings

Community property is all of the property acquired by either husband or wife during the marriage, except for property that is defined above as Separate property.

Money earned by a spouse during the marriage is considered to be community property, with an important distinction. Whoever earns the money has the right to the sole management and control of that money. A spouse also has the right to the sole management and control of anything he/she, alone, would have owned if he or she were single, that is:

⇨ the spouse's personal earnings

⇨ income derived from separate property

⇨ lost wages received as a result of a
    personal injury settlement

⇨ any increase in value from any of the above

⇨ any revenue received from any of the above

If the spouse mixes any of the above property with the rest of the couple's community property, then it becomes joint community property, that is, both partners have the right to spend and manage that property (Family 3.102).

CONVERTING COMMUNITY PROPERTY

A Texas couple can agree, in writing, to convert community property into separate property, provided, this is not done to protect assets from a creditor (Family 4.102).

Similarly, the couple can agree, in writing, to convert separate property to community property (Family 4.202). Many couples do this to obtain a favorable tax treatment. Under current tax law, when a spouse dies, all of their community property gets a step-up in basis. (IRC 1014(b)(6)). When one partner dies, all the community property is valued as of the decedent's date of death. If the surviving spouse sells the property at that time, then there is no capital gains tax. Prior to this time, the surviving spouse got a step-up in basis only on the half that was owned by the decedent.

COMMUNITY PROPERTY LIABILITY

If the surviving spouse agreed to be jointly responsible for the decedent's debt, then the surviving spouse must pay the debt from whatever assets he/she has, regardless of whether that property is separate property or community property. The surviving spouse is also liable if the debt was for the decedent's necessaries (food, clothing, shelter) (Family 2.501).

SPOUSE NOT RESPONSIBLE FOR FUNERAL EXPENSES

The spouse is not responsible to pay for the decedent's funeral expenses, nor for any burial plot or grave marker. These items are expenses charged to the decedent's estate (Probate Chap. VII, Sec. 320A). Of course if the spouse agrees to pay for the funeral (or any other debt) then the spouse must pay the monies owed.

Texas law requires the spouse to pay for the decedent's necessaries; but what if the decedent left business debts or an unpaid credit card that was in his name only?

If all the surviving spouse owns is separate property then the decedent's creditor cannot force the surviving spouse to use those assets to pay the debt. If there is joint community property available, then the surviving spouse must make that property available to pay his debts. If there is community property that was under the surviving spouse's sole control (such as wages held in a separate account), then those monies are not available to pay the decedent's debts, with one important exception. If the decedent did something wrong, and a judgment was placed against him during the marriage, then all community property — including community property that is under the surviving spouse's sole control, is available to pay that debt (Family 3.202).

SIGNIFICANT DEBT AND COMMUNITY PROPERTY ONLY

If the decedent left a significant amount of debt and only community property, then it is important to consult with an attorney. Theoretically, if the decedent came into the marriage with nothing and contributed little, then there may be little, if any, joint community property available to pay his debts. No doubt a creditor will not see things that way. Regardless of the amount of the decedent's contribution it is best to consult with a Probate attorney to determine what liability is left to the surviving spouse.

Special Situation > NO COMMUNITY LIABILITY FOR MEDICAID

Medicaid is a program that provides medical and long term nursing care for people with low income and limited resources. The program is funded jointly by the federal and state government. Federal law 42 U.S.C. 1396(p) requires the state to put into effect a plan to recover monies spent from the estate of a deceased Medicaid recipient. If the decedent received long term medical assistance after he became 65, then the federal government requires the state of Texas to seek to recovery for monies spent on his behalf. The federal government does not require the state to seek recovery if the decedent has a surviving spouse, or a child who is disabled, or a child who is under 21.

JOINT DEBTS

A *joint debt* is a debt that two or more people are responsible to pay. Usually the contract or promissory note reads that both parties agree to *joint and severable* liability, meaning they both agree to pay the debt and each of them, individually, agree to be pay the debt. A joint debt can also be in the form of monies owed by one person with payment guaranteed by another person. If the person who owes the money does not pay, then the *guarantor* is responsible to pay the debt.

Before paying a bill, determine whether it is the decedent's debt or a joint debt. Hospital bills, nursing home bills, funeral expenses, legal fees incurred because of the decedent's death are all debts of the decedent's estate. They are not joint debts unless someone guaranteed payment for the monies owed.

DEBTS THE SPOUSE MUST PAY
Loans signed by the decedent and his spouse are joint debts, as are charges on credit cards that both were authorized to use. Property taxes are a joint debt if the decedent and the spouse both owned the property.

PAYING FOR THE JOINT DEBT
If another person is jointly responsible for monies owed by the decedent, then that bill should be paid from any joint account held with the decedent. If the joint debtor did not have a joint account with the decedent, then the joint debtor must pay the bill from his/her own funds.

JOINT ACCOUNTS BUT NO JOINT DEBT

Suppose all of the decedent's funds are held *jointly with rights of survivorship* with a family member and the joint owner of the account did not agree to pay those debts? Can the creditor require that some of the joint funds be set aside to pay the debt? In Texas, the answer is "Yes." Texas statute (Probate Chap. XI, Sec. 442) states that if there isn't enough money in the decedent's estate to pay all of his creditors and/or the statutory allowances to the surviving spouse and children, then the joint owner must give the money from the decedent's share of a joint account to the decedent's Personal Representative to the extent those monies are needed to pay such debts. The decedent's share of the account is determined by how much the decedent actually contributed to that account.

Similarly, if the decedent had an account and he gave written instructions to the bank to pay the money to a beneficiary when he dies (a *"pay on death"* or an *"in trust for"* account) then those funds can also be used to pay the decedent's creditors.

If the joint owner or beneficiary of the account takes the decedent's share of the account and it is needed to pay the decedent's debts, then as much as is necessary to pay the debt must be returned. There is no obligation to turn over these funds unless the spouse or a creditor writes to the Personal Representative demanding that the monies from the account be used to pay the debt. Once the Personal Representative receives the demand, then unless the beneficiary agrees to return the funds, the Personal Representative will start a court proceeding to recover the funds. The Personal Representative has two years from the date of death to start such action, so if there is no court proceeding within two years from the decedent's date of death, the beneficiary is free to keep the money.

NO MONEY — NO PROPERTY

If the decedent owed money then his bills need to be paid from the probate estate of the decedent — which leads to the next question "Did the decedent have any money in his name only when he died?"

If the decedent died without any money or property then there is no money to pay any creditor. The only question that remains is whether anyone else is liable to pay those bills. As discussed previously, if the decedent was married then the creditor can look to community property held by the surviving spouse for payment. If the decedent was single, or if there is no community property, then the creditor has no means of being paid, but that usually does not stop them from asking for payment from the family.

The issue of payment most often arises in relation to services provided by nursing homes. When a person enters a nursing home, he is usually too ill to speak for himself or even sign his name. In such cases, the nursing home administrator will ask the spouse or a family member to sign a battery of papers on behalf of the patient before allowing the patient to enter the facility. Buried in that battery of papers may be a statement that the family member agrees to be responsible for payment to the nursing home. If the family member refuses to guarantee payment and the patient's finances are limited, then the facility may refuse to admit the patient.

If a nursing home accepts Medicare or Medicaid payments, then under the Federal Nursing Home Reform Law, that nursing home is prohibited from requiring a family member to guarantee payment as a condition of allowing the patient to enter that facility. USC Title 42 §1395I-3(c)(5)(A)(ii). Nonetheless, it is common practice for a nursing home, in effect, to say "Either someone agrees to pay for the patient's bill or you need to find a different facility."

Their position is understandable. Most nursing homes are business establishments and not charitable organizations. The nursing home must be paid for the services they provide or they soon will be out of business. For an insolvent patient, the solution to the problem is to have the patient admitted to a facility as a Medicaid patient.

But what if the decedent had some money when he entered the nursing home and you agreed to guarantee payment to the nursing home?

What if you feel that you were coerced into signing as a guarantor?

Are you now liable to pay the decedent's final nursing home bill if your family member died without funds?

An experienced Elder Law attorney will be able to answer these questions after examining the documents that you signed and the conditions under which the patient entered the nursing home.

AN ESTATE WITH ASSETS

If the decedent owed money and he died owning property, belonging to him alone, such as a bank account, securities, or real property, then there may be money available to pay monies owed by the decedent. It is up to the decedent's Personal Representative to pay all valid debts, but to do so the Personal Representative first must gain possession of the decedent's assets. To gain possession of the decedent's assets, there will need to be some sort of probate procedure to determine who is entitled to the decedent's property.

Once the probate procedure begins, all of the decedent's creditors will be given an opportunity to come forward and produce evidence showing how much is owed. The Personal Representative needs to look over each unpaid invoice and decide whether it is a valid bill. The problem with making that decision is that the decedent is not here to say whether he actually received the goods and services now being billed to his estate.

That is especially the case for medical or nursing care bills. An example of improper billing brought to the attention of this author was that of a bill submitted for a physical examination of the decedent. The bill listed the date of the examination as July 10th, but the decedent died on July 9th. Other incorrect billings may not be as obvious, so each invoice needs to be carefully examined.

If the Personal Representative decides to challenge a bill, and is unable to settle the matter with the creditor, then the probate court will decide whether the debt is valid and should be paid.

MEDICAL BILLS COVERED BY INSURANCE

If the decedent had health insurance you may receive an invoice stamped "THIS IS NOT A BILL." This means that the health care provider has submitted the bill to the decedent's health insurance company and expects to be paid by them. Even though payment is not requested, it is important that you verify that the bill is valid for two reasons:

➤ LATER LIABILITY

If the insurer refuses to pay the claim, the facility will seek payment from whoever is in possession of the decedent's property, and that may reduce the amount inherited by the beneficiaries.

➤ INCREASED HEALTH CARE COSTS

Regardless of whether the decedent was covered by a private health care insurer or Medicare, improper billing increases the cost of health insurance to all of us. Consumers pay high premiums for health coverage. We, as taxpayers, all share the cost of Medicare. If unnecessary or fraudulent billing is not checked, then ultimately, we all pay.

 MEDICARE FRAUD

If you believe that you have come across a case of Medicare fraud, you can call the ANTI-FRAUD HOTLINE (800) 447-8477 and report the incident to the Office of the Inspector General of the United States Department of Health and Human Services.

HOW TO CHECK MEDICARE BILLING

If the decedent was covered by Medicare, then an important billing question is whether the health care provider agreed to accept Medicare *assignment of benefits*, meaning that they agreed to accept payment directly from Medicare. If so, the maximum liability for the patient is **20%** of the amount determined as reasonable by Medicare. For example, suppose a doctor bills Medicare $1,000 for medical treatment of the decedent. If Medicare determines that a reasonable fee is $800, then the patient is liable for 20% of the $800 ($160).

Health care providers who do not accept Medicare assignment, bill the patient directly. They can charge up to 15% more than the amount allowed by Medicare. If the decedent knew and agreed to be liable for the payment, then his estate may be liable for whatever Medicare doesn't pay. For example, if a doctor's bill is $1,000 and Medicare allows $800, then Medicare will reimburse the decedent's estate 80% of $800 ($640). The doctor may charge the estate 15% more than the $800 ($920) and the estate may be liable for the difference: $920 - $640 or $280.

To summarize:
For health care providers accepting Medicare assignment, the most they can bill the decedent's estate is 20% of what Medicare allows (not 20% of what they bill.)

Those who do not accept Medicare assignment, can bill 15% more than the amount allowed by Medicare. The decedent's estate may be liable for the difference between the amount billed and the amount paid by Medicare.

In either case, if the decedent had secondary health care insurance, then the secondary insurer may be responsible to pay for the difference. If you have a question about Medicare billing call MEDICARE PART B CUSTOMER SERVICE: (800) 333-7586.

DENIAL OF
MEDICARE COVERAGE

If the health care provider reports to you that services provided to the decedent are not covered by Medicare, or if the facility submits the bill to Medicare and Medicare refuses to pay, then check to see if you agree with that ruling by determining what services are covered under Medicare. See page 45 of this book for information about how to obtain pamphlets that explain what medical treatments are covered under Medicare.

If you believe that the decedent has wrongly been denied coverage, then you can appeal that decision. Texas has some 28 Area Agencies On Aging offices throughout the state to assist you. You can call the Texas Department on Aging at (800) 252-2412 and they will give you the telephone number of the Agency On Aging office nearest you.

If you wish to have an attorney assist with your appeal you can call the Texas Bar (800) 252-9690 for a referral to an attorney experienced in Medicare appeals. Some attorneys work *pro bono* (literally for the public good; i.e. without charge) but most charge to assist in an appeal. Federal statute limits the amount an attorney may charge for a successful Medicare appeal to 25% of the amount recovered or $4,000, whichever is the smaller amount (42 U.S.C. §406(a)(2)(A)).

SOME THINGS ARE CREDITOR PROOF

Sometimes it happens that the decedent had money or property titled in his name only but he also had a significant amount of debt. In such cases the beneficiaries may wonder whether they should go through a probate procedure if there will be little, if anything, left after creditors are paid. Before coming to that conclusion consider that some assets are protected by Texas statute:

✧ THE HOMESTEAD EXEMPTION ✧

Texas property owned and occupied by a person as his/her main residence is called *homestead* property. Texas statute protects the homestead from forced sale by creditors. Should the owner of the homestead die, then creditor protection of his home, continues to his spouse or family members who inherit the homestead (Probate Chap. VIII, Sec. 270; Property 41.001).

There are exceptions to this rule. Creditor protection does not extend to delinquent taxes or mortgages on the homestead or to mechanics' liens. But in general, if all that the decedent owned was his homestead, the decedent's creditors will not be able to force the sale of the homestead to pay those debts.

This exemption is unlimited, meaning that if the homestead is worth a million dollars, then essentially one million dollars of the decedent's estate is creditor proof. There is a bill being considered in the United States Congress, which if passed, would limit a homestead exemption, to $100,000, but as of this writing, in Texas, the homestead exemption is unlimited.

✧ PERSONAL PROPERTY EXEMPTION ✧

In the state of Texas, certain personal items are exempt from the claims of creditors. Unlike the homestead exemption, there is a limit on the value of the protected items. For a single adult, the protected amount is $30,000 for a family, the amount is $60,000. Exempt personal property includes:

⇨ home furnishings, including family heirlooms

⇨ items used in a trade or profession including tools, books, farming equipment, certain farm animals, etc.

⇨ two firearms

⇨ clothing, athletic and sporting equipment

⇨ motor vehicles and bicycles

⇨ jewelry, not to exceed 25% of the protected amount

⇨ unpaid commissions for personal services, not to exceed 25% of the protected amount

This exemption does not apply to monies owned on a given item, for example, a car loan must be paid, or the creditor can take the car (Property 42.001, 42.002).

✧ OTHER EXEMPT PROPERTY ✧

The following items are also exempt but they are not counted as part of the protected amount; i.e., these items have no dollar limit and they are exempt, in addition to all other exempt items:

⇨ a burial lot

⇨ final wages for decedent's personal services

⇨ professionally prescribed health aids for the decedent or any of his dependents

⇨ alimony or support payments for the decedent or any of his dependents (Property 42.001 (a), (b)).

The decedent's spouse and children have the right to inherit the exempt items listed on this page, free of creditor's claims. If the decedent left neither spouse nor child then these items are available to pay claims.

✧ RETIREMENT PLANS ✧

Any retirement plan, including:

⇨   IRA accounts

⇨   annuity retirement contracts

⇨   federal retirement plans 401(a), 403 a & b, 408 A, 409

⇨   deferred plans under section 457 of the
          US Internal Revenue Code

are exempt from the claims of creditors (Property 42.0021).

All monies received by beneficiaries of these plans are protected from the decedent's creditors — even from the income tax claims on these monies from other states; i.e., if monies were earned by the decedent in another state, that state cannot make an income tax claim on the decedent's pension funds that are distributed in the state of Texas (Property 44.003).

✧ LIFE INSURANCE PROCEEDS ✧

If the life of the decedent was insured, then the beneficiary of the policy can keep the proceeds of the policy. Regardless of the amount of the insurance, the decedent's creditors cannot make any claim to the proceeds of the insurance policy (Insurance 21.22).

✧ THE FAMILY ALLOWANCE ✧

The probate court can order the Personal Representative to set aside sufficient funds for the support of the decedent's spouse and/or minor children while the estate is being probated. The amount is set by the court and is based on the amount needed for up to a year from the date of death. The monies can be paid in a single lump sum, or in the form of a monthly allowance. The court will not award any allowance if the spouse and/or minor child have sufficient assets for their own support (Probate Chap. VIII, Sec. 286, 287, 288).

✧ THERE IS A STATUTE OF LIMITATION ✧

A *statute of limitation* is a law that sets a maximum time period during which a person can sue to enforce a right. After the time period runs, the person is barred from taking any legal action on the matter. The statute of limitation for a creditor to bring a claim against the Probate Estate depends to a great deal on whether the Personal Representative gave written notice to the creditor that the decedent is dead, and where to file a claim.

Texas law requires that, within one month after receiving Letters that give him authority to act, the Personal Representative publish notice in the county newspaper giving the name and address where claims can be presented. He is also required to give written notice to any creditor having a *secured claim* i.e., a claim that is backed by some item (usually a house or car) that the creditor can take should the debt be in default. The lender might decide to allow the new owner of the property to take over the loan, provided the new owner agrees to be personally liable for the payments. If the lender does not allow the assignment of the loan to the beneficiary, then the entire balance becomes due and payable and the loan is said to have "*matured.*"

A secured creditor has 6 months after the Letters are issued to come forward and request that the loan be treated as a mature loan. If the creditor neglects to do so, then the estate has no duty to pay off the balance of the loan, and it then becomes the beneficiary's responsibility to see that the loan is paid (Probate Chap. VIII, Sec. 306).

✧ STATUTE OF LIMITATION FOR UNSECURED CLAIMS ✧

An *unsecured creditor* is someone who is owed money, but with no tangible item that the creditor can take in the event of default. Credit card debts, telephone bills, personal loans and personal guarantees are usually unsecured debts. Texas law does not require the Personal Representative to give written notice to an unsecured creditor, but it is important to the beneficiaries that he do so. If the Personal Representative gives the unsecured creditor written notice, then that creditor has exactly four months to come forward and make a claim for monies owed. If he doesn't come forward during that time, then his claim is forever barred (Probate Chap. VIII, Sec. 294).

If the Personal Representative fails to give notice to the unsecured creditor, then the creditor can place a claim against the estate at any time. If the estate has been closed and the property distributed, then the creditor can sue any of the people who inherited property from the estate, up to the value of the property that they inherited (Probate Chap.VIII, Sec. 269 and Sec. 318).

There is general statute of limitations for each type of claim. For example, if the decedent signed a lease and the landlord was not given written notice from the Personal Representative, then the landlord has 4 years from the time the default occurred to sue the beneficiaries for monies due under the lease. That time period could be even longer because Texas law puts the statute of limitations on hold for 12 months or until a Personal Representative is appointed whichever happens sooner (Civ. Prac. & Rem. 16.062 and Bus. & Com. 2A.506).

To prevent later headaches, it is important that the Personal Representative give every known creditor written notice, so that the creditor must file the claim against the estate within 4 months of receiving that notice or lose his right to be paid.

✧ THERE IS A PRIORITY OF PAYMENT ✧

Not all probate debts are equal. Texas statute establishes an order of priority for payment of claims made against the decedent's estate:

CLASS 1: FUNERAL EXPENSES

Top priority are the decedent's reasonable funeral expenses and the expenses of his last illness in an amount not to exceed $15,000. Anything in excess of $15,000 becomes an unsecured, Class 8 debt.

FAMILY ALLOWANCE

If the Probate court allows a Family Allowance then only Class 1 Funeral Expenses have priority over the Family Allowance.

CLASS 2: COSTS OF ADMINISTRATION

The cost of the probate procedure including filing fees, the cost of managing and preserving the decedent's estate, attorney's fees and fees charged by the Personal Representative.

CLASS 3: SECURED CLAIMS

If a secured claim (including any tax lien on the decedent's property) is determined by the probate court to be a matured claim, then that claim is third in priority of payment.

CLASS 4: DELINQUENT CHILD SUPPORT

If a court has ruled that the decedent owed monies for back child support, then payment of that judgment is fourth in priority of payment.

CLASS 5: TAXES

If the decedent owned any monies for taxes, including penalties and interest on those taxes, then these become a class 4 claim against the estate.

CLASS 6: THE COST OF JAIL

If the decedent was confined in Texas correctional institution at the time of his death, then the state of Texas has a right to file a claim against his estate for monies spent for his care while in the facility. The state of Texas will not file the claim if the decedent had a surviving spouse, or a dependent or disabled child (Government 501.017).

CLASS 7: MEDICAL ASSISTANCE PAYMENT

The state has the right to be reimbursed for government funds spent on the decedent medical care during his lifetime. Usually there are no monies to recover because to qualify for Medicaid in Texas, a person may not have more than $2,000 in assets. But sometimes it happens that a person on Medicaid dies and his estate later receives money perhaps as part of a cash settlement of a lawsuit. In such case, the state of Texas becomes a Class 6 creditor, having priority above the rest of the decedent's creditors (Human Resources 32.033).

CLASS 8: ALL OTHER CLAIMS

If any money is left after all the prior classes are paid, then the Personal Representative will use it to pay all of the decedent's valid debts. All the debtors in this class have the same right to be paid. If there is not enough money to pay all of the creditors, then the Personal Representative will prorate the available funds (Probate Chap. VIII, Sec. 322).

MONIES OWED TO THE DECEDENT

Suppose you owed money to the decedent? Do you need to pay that debt now that he is dead? That depends on whether there is some written document that says the debt is forgiven once the decedent dies. For example, suppose the decedent lent you money to buy your home. If he left a Will saying that once he dies, your debt is forgiven, then you do not need to make any more payments. If you signed a promissory note and mortgage at the time you borrowed the money from the decedent, then the Personal Representative should sign the original promissory note "PAID IN FULL" and return the note to you. If the mortgage was recorded, then the Personal Representative should sign and record a satisfaction of mortgage.

If you owed the decedent money and there is no Will, or if there is a Will and no mention of forgiving the debt, then you still owe the money. You need to continue to make payments. If you borrowed the money from the decedent and his spouse, then you will pay the money to the spouse. If you borrowed the money from the decedent only, then the debt becomes an asset to the estate of the decedent, meaning that you now owe the money to his heirs. If you are one of those heirs, you can deduct the money from your inheritance.

For example, suppose your father left $70,000 in a bank account to be divided equally between you and your two brothers. If you owe your father $20,000, then your father's estate is really worth $90,000. Your share of the inheritance is $30,000. Instead of paying the $20,000, you can agree to receive $10,000 and have the $20,000 debt forgiven. Each of your brothers will then receive their $30,000 in cash.

Who Are The Beneficiaries? 5

A question that comes up early on is who is entitled to the property of the decedent. To answer the question you first need to know how the property was titled (owned) as of the date of death.

There are three ways to own property. The decedent could have owned property jointly with another person; or in trust for another person; or the decedent could have owned property that was titled in his name only.

In general, upon the decedent's death:

Joint Property with rights of survivorship belongs to the surviving joint owner.

Trust Property belongs to the beneficiary of the trust.

Property owned by the **decedent only** belongs to the beneficiaries named in the Will.
If there is no Will, then the property goes to his heirs according to the Texas Law of Descent and Distribution.

NOTE ⇨ If the decedent was married, then his spouse may have rights in his property.

This chapter explains each of these types of ownership in detail.

PROPERTY HELD JOINTLY

Bank accounts, securities, motor vehicles, real property can all be owned jointly by two or more people. If one of the joint owners dies, then the survivor(s) continue to own their own share of the property. Who owns the share belonging to the decedent depends on how the joint ownership was set up:

THE JOINT BANK ACCOUNT

If two or more people open a bank account, then it is called a *joint account*. During their lifetime, each person named on the account, is entitled to as much as they contributed unless there is clear evidence of a different intent. (Probate Chap. XI, Sec. 438 (a)).

When a joint account is set up, the people opening the account sign a document (contract or signature card or passbook) saying who is to own the account if one of the owners of the account dies. An account can be set up with or without the right of the surviving owners to inherit the monies in the account. There are no rights of survivorship unless the account specifically say so. Even community property accounts between husband and wife have no right of survivorship unless the account contract states:
"with right of survivorship"
— or —
"shall pass to the surviving spouse"
— or —
"will become the property of the survivor"
(Probate Chap. II, Sec. 46 and Chap. XI, Sec. 440, Sec. 451 and Sec. 452)

RIGHT OF SURVIVORSHIP

If a joint account is set up with a right of survivorship, and one of the owners dies, then the remaining owner(s) own the account. A joint account can be set up so that there is a specific beneficiary to the account once they all die. If no beneficiary is named, then when the last owner of the account dies, the funds become part of his estate. If the last joint owner to die leaves a Will, the money in the account goes to the beneficiaries named in the Will. If he died without a Will then the money is distributed according to the Texas Law of Descent and Distribution (See page 106).

THE CONVENIENCE ACCOUNT

If the decedent needed assistance with his finances, he may have added someone to his bank or securities account for his own convenience and not with the intent of giving that person any right to the monies in the account. If that is the case, then the name on the account should reflect that intent, for example:

ALFRED RAY and ENID RAY, for the convenience of ALFRED RAY

This is not a joint account. The account is the same as if it were held in Alfred's name only. Once Alfred dies the account becomes part of Alfred's estate and Enid no longer has the right to transact business with this account. Just as soon as the bank is notified of the death, they will freeze the account until they receive notice of who has the legal authority to access the account (Probate Chap. XI, Sec. 438A).

JOINTLY HELD SECURITIES

The same rules apply to securities accounts that are held jointly. If the stock or bond is held jointly with right of survivorship and an owner dies, then the security belongs to the remaining owner. If the security is held as *tenants-in-common*, then if one owner dies, his share goes to the beneficiary named in his Will (or if no Will, then according the Law of Descent and Distribution) and not to the joint owner.

SECURITIES ISSUED IN OTHER STATES

Each state has its own laws regulating securities issued in that state. If the security was issued in another state, then how the account was set up will determine who inherits the property once the owner dies. An inspection of the face of a securities certificate may not always reveal how the security was purchased. For example, if two names are printed on the certificate with no other notation, it could mean that the security was purchased as joint tenants with rights of survivorship or as tenants-in-common. You need to contact the company and ask them how the account was set up, and also to request the necessary forms to either cash in the security or change the certificate to identify the new owner.

BROKERAGE ACCOUNTS

If the decedent held securities in a brokerage account then the name of the owner of that account is printed on the monthly or quarterly brokerage statement. Not all brokerage houses include the name of the joint owner on the brokerage statement so you need to contact the brokerage house and request a copy of the contract that is the basis of the account. If you determine that the account is held jointly or for the benefit of someone, then have the brokerage firm forward the necessary forms to make the transfer to the proper owner or beneficiary.

JOINTLY HELD MOTOR VEHICLES

If a motor vehicle is held jointly, the name of each owner is printed on the title to the motor vehicle, for example:

MARY SMITH, HENRY SMITH

If one of the parties dies, then some sort of Probate procedure is necessary to determine who now owns the decedent's share of the car. The Probate procedure is necessary, even if the couple is married. See Chapter 6 for a discussion of the Probate procedure.

If the owners of the motor vehicle intended the other to inherit the car should one of them die, then title to the car should reflect that fact, such as:

MARY SMITH, HENRY SMITH
WITH RIGHTS OF SURVIVORSHIP

Should one of them die, then the other is the sole owner of the car. The surviving owner should go to their local County Tax Assessor-Collectors office and have title to the car changed to his/her name only. See page 138 for information about how to transfer the title.

It is prudent to change title just as soon as is practicable. You might be able to get a reduced insurance rate if there is only one person insured under the policy. Also, should you be involved in an accident, by changing title officially, then there is no question but that you are the sole owner and the estate of the decedent is in no way liable for the accident.

REAL PROPERTY

The name of the owner of real property is printed on the face of the deed. To determine whether the decedent owned the property jointly with another person, you need to look at the last recorded deed. (See page 60 if you cannot locate the deed.)

Once you have possession of the last recorded deed, look at the person who is named right after the phrase:
". . . does hereby grant to _____"
or the person named after the phrase:
". . . does hereby quitclaim to _____."

That person is the "GRANTEE." The Grantee is the owner of the property as of the date of the decedent's death.

 JOINT TENANTS WITH RIGHTS OF SURVIVORSHIP

If the deed identifies the Grantee as the decedent and another person as **JOINT TENANTS WITH RIGHTS OF SURVIVORSHIP** then upon the decedent's death, the surviving tenants own the property. If you are the surviving owner, you do not need to do anything to establish that you now own the property, but the decedent's name still remains on the deed.

When you are someday ready to sell, you can show the death certificate to the title company to satisfy them that you are now the owner of the property with full authority to transfer the property.

📄 DEED HELD AS HUSBAND AND WIFE

In many states, a deed held as husband and wife, means that the surviving partner owns the property. This is not the case in Texas because Texas is a community property state. In Texas, it is presumed that a parcel held as husband and wife is community property with each partner owning half. When one partner dies his share is part of his estate and does not automatically descend to his spouse. If the parties want the surviving partner to own all of the property then the deed needs to state this, for example, TODD AMES AND SUSAN AMES,
AS COMMUNITY PROPERTY
WITH RIGHT OF SURVIVORSHIP.

If the deed states that the spouse has the right of survivorship, then when the spouse sells the property, all the spouse need do to establish that he/she is the sole owner is to present the buyer with a certified copy of the decedent's death certificate.

 **LAWYER**

DIVORCED PRIOR TO DEATH

If the decedent was divorced before he died, and he still holds property together with his ex-spouse, then unless the Final Judgment of Dissolution states otherwise, all property held by the couple in joint tenancy is considered as community property with each person owning half the property (Family 3.003). The decedent's half of the property will descend to his heirs or beneficiaries and not to his former spouse. You may need the assistance of a Probate attorney to have a new deed issued that identifies the owners of the decedent's share of the property.

▤   DEED HELD AS TENANTS IN COMMON

If the Grantee section of a deed identifies the decedent and another person as TENANTS IN COMMON then the decedent's share of the property belongs to whomever the decedent named as his beneficiary in his Will. If the decedent died without a Will, then the Texas Law of Descent and Distribution determines who inherits the decedent's share. See page 106 for an explanation of the law.

If property is owned by the decedent as a Tenant In Common, then a probate procedure is necessary. The next chapter describes the type of probate procedure that is necessary in order to establish who is the owner of the decedent's share of the property.

   LAWYER   THE AMBIGUOUS DEED

Most deeds clearly state whether the joint owners of the property intend a surviving owner to inherit the decedents share. For example:
DAN ROGOW and ANN ROGOW, as Tenants In Common
means that there are no rights of survivorship.
But DAN ROGOW and ANN ROGOW as Joint Tenants   or
      DAN ROGOW and ANN ROGOW, his wife   or
      DAN ROGOW and ANN ROGOW, jointly
are not all that clear.

According to Texas law, no right of survivorship exists unless the document clearly states so. That being the case, each of the above examples have no right of survivorship. They are the same as a tenancy-in-common (Probate Chap. II, Sec. 46). If you have any question about how to interpret a deed, it is best to consult with an attorney.

🗐 DEED WITH A LIFE ESTATE

A *Life Estate interest* in real property means that the person who owns the Life Estate interest has the right to live in that property until he/she dies. While the owner of the Life Estate is alive, the Grantee has no right to occupy the property. Once the owner of the Life Estate dies, the *remainder interest* belongs to the person who is named as Grantee on the deed.

You can identify a Life Estate interest by examining the face of the deed. If somewhere on the face of the deed you see the phrase RESERVING A LIFE ESTATE to the decedent then the Grantee now owns the property. For example, suppose the granting paragraph of the deed reads:

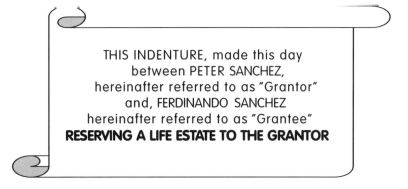

THIS INDENTURE, made this day
between PETER SANCHEZ,
hereinafter referred to as "Grantor"
and, FERDINANDO SANCHEZ
hereinafter referred to as "Grantee"
RESERVING A LIFE ESTATE TO THE GRANTOR

Once Peter dies, Ferdinando owns and has the right to occupy the property. Ferdinando should keep a certified copy of the death certificate available to present to the buyer in the event he later decides to sell the property.

PROPERTY HELD IN TRUST

BANK/ SECURITY ACCOUNTS

If a bank account is held in the name of the decedent "in trust for" or "for the benefit of" someone, then once the bank has a certified copy of the death certificate, the bank will turn over the account to the beneficiary. Similarly, if the decedent held a security or a securities brokerage account "in trust for" someone, then upon receipt of the death certificate, that account becomes the property of the beneficiary (Probate, Chap. XI, Sec. 439(c)).

If the bank or security account is registered in the name of the decedent "as trustee under a trust agreement," that means the decedent was the trustee of a trust and the bank will turn over that account to the Successor Trustee of the trust. Banks usually require a copy of the trust when the account was opened, so the bank probably knows the identity of the Successor Trustee. If the trust was amended to name a different Successor Trustee, you need to present the bank with a copy of that amendment together with a certified copy of the death certificate (Property 112.084).

MOTOR VEHICLE

If the motor vehicle is held in the name of the decedent "as trustee under a trust agreement," then the motor vehicle is part of the trust property. The motor vehicle remains in the trust once the decedent trustee dies. The Successor Trustee will need to contact the your local Tax Assessor Collector's Office to correct the name on the title. See page 137 for the number of the Texas Department of Transportation. They can give you telephone numbers for your local Tax Assessor Collector's Office.

REAL PROPERTY HELD IN TRUST

If the decedent had a trust and put property that he owned into the trust then the deed may read something like this:

THIS INDENTURE
made this day between
JOHN ZAMORA and MARIA ZAMORA, his wife,
hereinafter referred to as "Grantor",
and
JOHN ZAMORA **trustee of the**
JOHN ZAMORA TRUST AGREEMENT
DATED February 2, 2000,
hereinafter referred to as "Grantee"

Once the trustee (John Zamora) dies then that property remains in the trust. The trust document will say whether the person who takes John's place as trustee (the *Successor Trustee*) should sell or keep the property or perhaps give it to a beneficiary. If no instruction is given, then what the Successor Trustee does with the property may be affected by laws relating to the administration of trust property in the state where the property is located. If you are a beneficiary of the trust and you are concerned about what the Successor Trustee will do with the property, then it is best to consult with your attorney.

| SPOUSE | AN INVISIBLE LIFE ESTATE |

If the decedent was married and the deed to his homestead was in the decedent's name, then Texas law gives the spouse the right to live in that home until he/she dies. Once the spouse dies, then whoever inherits the property can take possession of the property. Similarly, if the decedent is survived by a minor child, then the guardian of the child has the right to ask the Probate court to allow the child to occupy the property until the child is an adult (Probate Chap. VIII, Sec. 283 - 286).

| ☎ LAWYER | OUT OF STATE DEED |

This chapter relates only to property owned by the decedent in the state of Texas. If the decedent owned property in another state or country, then the laws of that state or country (and maybe even the laws of Texas) will determine who inherits the property. You need to consult with an attorney in that state to determine who owns the property now that the Grantee is dead.

 INVALID DEED

The discussion on the different types of ownership of real property presumes that you are in possession of the most recent, valid, deed. The decedent could have signed a different deed after the deed you have in your possession. Before you come to a conclusion about who inherits the property it is advisable to have an attorney, or a title company, do a title search to determine the owner of the property as of the decedent's date of death.

PROPERTY IN DECEDENT'S NAME ONLY

If the decedent owned property that was in his name only (not jointly with rights of survival, or in trust for someone) then we identify that property as the decedent's **Probate Estate**. We call it the Probate Estate because some sort of probate procedure will be necessary before anyone can get possession of that property. Who is entitled to the decedent's Probate Estate depends on whether the decedent died with or without a Will. If the decedent died testate, then the Will states who is to receive the property. If a person neglects to write a Will then the state provides one for him in the form of the Texas Law of Descent and Distribution (Probate Chap.II, Sec. 38).

Texas is a community property state so if the decedent was a resident of Texas and he was married, then the Texas Law of Descent and Distribution applies to the decedent's separate property and his half community property. We identify a **married decedent's intestate property** as:

⇨ all of his separate property

⇨ half of the couple's community property

As discussed earlier, a married couple have the right to create a right of survivorship in any of their community property, but for purposes of this discussion, when we use the term "community property," we assume that the couple had no written agreement to distribute that property any differently than according to the Texas Law of Descent and Distribution.

THE LAW OF DESCENT AND DISTRIBUTION

Texas recognizes the right of the family to inherit the decedent's property, so if a resident of Texas dies without a Will his property is passed to his next of kin according to the Texas Law of Descent and Distribution:

SINGLE, WITH CHILDREN

If the decedent was not married at the time of his death and he had children, then they inherit his property in equal shares. This is easy to understand if all of the decedent's children survive him. But suppose one of his children dies before he does? What happens to the share intended for that child? According to Texas law, if the deceased child left *descendants* (children, grandchildren, etc.), then they take that share. If the deceased child did not leave descendants, then the surviving children divide the inheritance (Probate Chap. II, Sec. 43).

For example:

ALL CHILDREN SURVIVE

Suppose the decedent was unmarried with 4 children, Ann, Barry, Carl, David and he died without a Will, then each of his children get 25% of his estate.

CHILD WITHOUT DESCENDANTS DIES BEFORE DECEDENT

If Ann dies before her father, leaving no descendants, then Barry, Carl and David divide the estate between them. Each gets one third of the estate.

CHILDREN WITH DESCENDANTS DIES BEFORE DECEDENT

Suppose instead that only Carl and David survive their father. If Ann died leaving no children and Barry died leaving 2 children, then the estate is divided into 3 shares — one for each surviving child (Carl and David) and one share for Barry's children, who split their share equally.

The thing to remember is that the initial division takes place at the nearest generation with living members. For example, if the decedent had only surviving grand-children, then his property is divided into as many shares as grandchildren. If a grandchild died, leaving a great-grandchild, then the property is divided in the same manner as described for children. The legal term to describe this method of distributing property is called *per stirpes*.

SINGLE, NO CHILDREN

If the decedent was single and without children then his estate goes in equal shares to his parents. If only one parent survives him, then that parent gets half and the decedent's brothers and sisters get the other half, in equal shares, per stirpes. If there are no brothers or sisters (or their descendants), then the surviving parent receives the entire Probate estate.

If neither parent survive him, then the brothers and sisters share the entire estate in equal shares, per stirpes. And if no brothers, or sisters (or their descendants) then the Probate estate is divided with half going to the relatives on the decedent's mother's side and half to the relatives on his father's side. For the actual break-down see Probate Chap. II, Section 38 (a)(4).

MARRIED, NO CHILDREN

If the decedent was married and had no surviving descendants or parent, or brother, sister, or descendants of a deceased brother or sister, then the spouse inherits all of the decedent's intestate property. If the decedent is survived by parent, sibling or descendants of siblings, then the decedent's family is entitled to one half of all of the decedent's separate real property which they inherit in same manner as if the decedent was single and without children (see prior page). The spouse inherits all the rest of the decedent's intestate estate. (Probate Chap. II, Sec. 38 (b)(2)).

MARRIED WITH DESCENDANTS

COMMUNITY PROPERTY: If the decedent was married and all the decedent's children are those of the surviving spouse then the spouse inherits all of the community property. If the decedent had one or more children, who are not those of the surviving spouse, then the decedent's children inherit half of the couple's community property in equal shares, per stirpes (Probate Chap. II, Sec. 45).

SEPARATE PROPERTY: If the decedent was survived by a spouse and descendants, then the spouse gets one-third of the decedent's separate personal property and a life estate in one-third of the decedent's separate real property. The remaining 2/3rds of the separate personal property; the remaining 2/3rds of the life estate, and the remainder interest in the life estate, all go to the decedent's children in equal shares, per stirpes (Probate Chap. II, Sec. 38 (b)(1)).

THE STATE: HEIR OF LAST RESORT

If a person dies without a Will and he has absolutely no surviving relatives, then the decedent's intestate estate goes to the state of Texas (Property 71.001).

HALF BLOOD INHERITS HALF

If there are relatives of the decedent, some of whole blood and some of half blood, then the relative of half blood inherit half as much. For example, suppose the decedent had a brother from the same set of parents, and his father later remarried and had a daughter with another woman. If the decedent dies without a Will and his only relatives are his brother and half-sister, then his brother will inherit 2/3rds of his Probate estate and his half-sister, a third. Of course, if it happened that both brother and sister were half-blood, then they would divide the property equally (Probate Chap. II, Sec. 41 (b)).

CAUTION — IT ISN'T ALL THAT SIMPLE

The explanation in this book of the Law of Descent and Distribution is abridged. Even though you may now know more about the Law than you ever wanted to know, there is much more. Unless the descent is straight forward, with the decedent leaving a surviving spouse and/or children, it is best to consult with an attorney before you decide who is entitled to the decedent's intestate estate.

And, even the matter of who can be considered to be the decedent's spouse, and who can inherit as his child, can be complicated, as you will see on the next page.

WHAT'S A SPOUSE? WHAT'S A CHILD?

The Law of Descent and Distribution is based on family relationships. Texas has laws relating to what is meant by the term *spouse* and what is meant by *child*:

THE INFORMAL MARRIAGE

If a man and woman are formally married (i.e. licensed to be married and then followed by a state recognized ceremony), then regardless of where the ceremony takes place, the state of Texas recognizes that marriage. But suppose the decedent was living together as man and wife but without benefit of any ceremony. Many states refer to this as a Common Law marriage. Most states do not recognize a Common Law Marriage as being a valid marriage. Texas recognizes a Common Law marriage provided it meets the requirements of what is defined in Texas as an *Informal Marriage*. An Informal Marriage is one in which:

- ♡ A man and woman, each over 18, agree to be married.
- ♡ After the agreement they live together in Texas as husband and wife.
- ♡ They tell everyone that they are married.

If a couple is Informally Married, they can formalize their marriage by going to their local county Clerk and signing a form entitled:
DECLARATION AND REGISTRATION OF INFORMAL MARRIAGE

Once the document is signed the county Clerk will sign a certificate stating the place and time that the Declaration was made. The Clerk will give the couple the original Declaration and send a copy to the Texas Bureau of Vital Statistics. If the decedent was Informally Married and signed a Declaration, then the surviving spouse has all the rights of a spouse under Texas law (Family 2.401, 2.402, 2.404).

PROVING THE COMMON LAW MARRIAGE

If the decedent had a Common Law marriage in another state, or if the decedent was Informally Married in Texas, and did not sign a Declaration, then the spouse may need to employ an attorney to prove to the Probate court that the surviving spouse has rights in the decedent's estate.

THE ADOPTED CHILD

An adopted child has the same right to inherit from an adoptive parent as does a natural child. The adoptive family has the same right to inherit from the adoptive child as they would from any natural child. For example, if the decedent was an adopted child and he dies without a Will and his only family is his adoptive brothers and sisters, then they will inherit his estate. His natural parents have no right to his estate. But here's a surprising thing, the adopted child still has the right to inherit from his natural parents. For example, suppose a woman gives up her child for adoption, and then later has another child. If the woman dies without a Will, as a resident of the state of Texas, then her adoptive child has just as much right to inherit as does the child not placed for adoption (Probate Chap. II, Sec. 40).

CHILD BORN OUT OF WEDLOCK

A child born out of wedlock has the same rights to inherit from his/her natural father as does one born in wedlock, provided:

☑ the decedent acknowledged the child as his own and signed a document to that effect.

— or —

☑ paternity is established by a court (Probate Chap. II, Sec. 42 (b)).

 **LAWYER** | **DECEDENT DENIED PATERNITY**

If the decedent denied his paternity, then it will take a court procedure to establish (or disprove) paternity. If the decedent died without a Will, then the child can ask the Probate court to determine his/her right to inherit the decedent's estate.

If you want to establish paternity, then you will probably face a court battle over the issue. You will need to consult with an attorney who is experienced in litigation. In this day of DNA testing, if the family plans to cremate the decedent, you may need to have your attorney move quickly to bar cremation until the matter is settled.

WHO DIED FIRST?

Texas statute requires that a heir survive the decedent by at least 120 hours (5 days) in order to inherit property under the Law of Descent and Distribution. If an heir does not live for at least 120 hours after the decedent's death, then the decedent's property is distributed as if the heir died first. This rule does not apply if an imposition of the 120 hour limit results in the state of Texas taking the decedent's property.

Similarly if property is owned jointly with rights of survivorship, then the rule applies if the joint owners die within 120 hours of each other. In such case, the property is divided equally, with each share being inherited by the joint owner as if he had outlived the other joint owner.

The rule also applies to life and accident insurance policies. If the person whose life is insured dies within 120 hours of the beneficiary of the policy, then the beneficiary is said to have died first and the insurance proceeds are given to the alternate beneficiary of the policy.

If the decedent left a Will, then unless the Will states differently, the 120 hour rule applies. For example, if the decedent left property to his son, and the son dies four days later, then the gift to his son will be distributed as if the son died first, unless the Will gives different instructions (Probate Chap. II, Sec. 47).

NO INSURANCE BENEFITS FOR KILLER

If the beneficiary of an insurance policy willfully brings about the death of the insured person, then the killer gets none of the proceeds of the insurance policy. The monies are given to the person named as alternate beneficiary of the policy — unless the alternate was an accomplice to the crime, in which case the insurance proceeds go to the nearest relative of the insured (Insurance Art. 21.23).

Similarly, if the decedent was entitled to a pension or annuity from the state of Texas, and the beneficiary of the pension or annuity is convicted of causing his death, then the benefits are paid to the alternate beneficiary. If there is no alternate beneficiary, then the monies are paid to the decedent's estate (Government 854.504).

Other than insurance or pension funds, there is no provision for forfeiture of benefits by a killer. If a person is convicted of willfully killing the decedent, and that person stands to inherit property either through the Law of Descent and Distribution, or as willed to him by the decedent, there is no Texas law that prohibits him from collecting his inheritance (Probate Chap. II, Sec. 41(d).

Of course the Personal Representative of the decedent's estate can sue the killer for a wrongful death, and in effect prohibit the killer from profiting from the act.

WHEN TO CHALLENGE A WILL

It is not uncommon for a family member to be unhappy with the way the decedent willed his property. If you are tempted to challenge a Will, first consider whether the Will is valid under the Texas law.

THE VALID WILL

In the state of Texas, a Will is presumed to be valid if at the time the decedent made the Will:

➢ he was at least 18 years of age, or if not 18, then a married person, or a member of the armed forces.

➢ he was of sound mind (Probate Chap. IV. Sec. 57).

The decedent is thought to have acted with *sound mind* if:

✓ he knew what he was doing (namely making a Will);

✓ he knew what property he had;

✓ he remembered and understood his relationship to his family members and how they would be affected by his Will;

✓ he was not suffering from a delusional mental disorder affecting his ability to distribute his property;

✓ he was not being unduly influenced by anyone; i.e., no one was coercing him to do what they wanted instead of what he wanted.

A person is free to make a gift to anyone he wishes, except he cannot make a gift in the Will to the attorney who prepares the Will, unless that attorney is related to the decedent (Probate Chap. IV, Sec. 58b).

THE UNWITNESSED WILL

As explained, the first job of the Probate court is the proving of the Will; i.e. the determination of whether the Will is valid. If the Will is in writing and signed by the Willmaker in the presence of at least 2 credible witnesses, then there should be no problem in having the Will accepted into Probate. But the decedent may have left a Will that he wrote in his own hand, with no one signing as a witness. Such a Will is called a *holographic Will.* Most states will not accept a holographic Will into probate. The problem with a holographic Will, is its authenticity. If no one saw the decedent sign the Will, it is hard to determine whether the Will was written by the decedent or is a forgery. A holographic Will can be probated in the state of Texas, but it will take a court procedure to prove that the Will is valid (Probate Chap. IV, Sec. 60).

 **LAWYER**   THE HOLOGRAPHIC WILL

If all the decedent left was a holographic Will, then you need to employ an attorney experienced in probate matters to present proof to the court that the Will is valid. If the court determines that the evidence presented is not sufficient to prove the validity of the Will, then the court will rule that the decedent died without a Will and use the Law of Descent and Distribution to determine who inherits the decedent's property.

THE VERBAL WILL

Picture a death bed scene. The elderly gentleman is surrounded by several family members. In a whisper, just audible enough to be heard, he says:

"Even though I am a wealthy man, I never got around to making a Will. You all have been good to me, but I did want my entire fortune to go to my nephew, Robert. He has been like a son to me."

Do you think Robert can inherit his Uncle's estate?

If this took place in the state of Texas, then Robert is in luck provided he can prove:

⇨ The statement was made at the decedent's home or where he lived for 10 days or more preceding the date of the Will. The statement can be made away from home if he was taken away sick and then died before he was able to return to his home.

⇨ There are three credible witnesses who testify that the decedent called on someone to take notice or to bear witness that this was his Will.

Considering that the family members stand to inherit a fortune under the Law of Descent and Distribution, we can agree that Robert's attorney has his work cut out for him.

And even if the attorney is able to prove that his case, Texas statute allows a verbal Will for personal property, only. If the uncle owned real property in the state of Texas, then his real property will be inherited according to the Texas laws of Descent and Distribution (Probate Chap. IV, Sec. 64 and Sec. 65).

THE WILL THAT IS CONTRARY TO LAW

If a Will is valid in the state of Texas, then the probate court makes every effort to carry out the intent of the decedent, unless the Will is contrary to the laws of the state. Such was the case with a Will that was properly drafted by Nancy.

Nancy was married to an emotional bully. She had difficulty asserting herself so she put up with a lot until her daughter became a teenager and Nancy was able to get a full time job to support them both. Soon after the divorce she met Alan. He was much like Nancy — not the arguing type. The match would have been perfect but for Nancy's daughter. She resented Alan's presence. She had a close relationship with their father and felt that Alan cut off any hope she had of her parents being reconciled.

The daughter's behavior toward Alan was less than cordial. Nancy dealt with the problem as she had with all problems she encountered in her life, namely by not acknowledging that the problem existed. Finally, Alan could take no more and he filed for divorce.

Nancy was devastated. She really loved Alan, but she was unable to put her needs before those of her daughter. A few years after the divorce, her daughter went off to a college in Massachusetts. A lonely Nancy called a lonely Alan and in no time they were back living together in Nancy's house. They subsequently remarried. They enjoyed their life together and even decided to start their own family. Because Nancy had the child so late in her life, there were many complications and she died a month after their son was born.

Nancy made a Will after Alan divorced her, giving all of her property (including the house) to her daughter. She never did get around to changing the Will once she remarried. No sooner was the funeral over, when Nancy's daughter came in and demanded that Alan vacate her mother's home. Alan was furious and went to his attorney.

"Don't I have any rights? And what about my newborn son — doesn't he have rights?"

"He sure does. Texas law provides that if a child is born after a Will is made, and that Will gives property to other children of the decedent, then unless the Will specifically states otherwise, the 'forgotten' child is entitled to share the gift. This means that your son is entitled to half of whatever your step-daughter inherits (Probate Chap. IV, Sec. 67 (1) (B)).

As for your rights, under Texas law you have the right to live in the homestead for the rest of your life. Once you die the house will be inherited equally by your son and step-daughter (Probate Chap.VIII, Sec. 284).

You do not need to pay for any of your wife's funeral expenses. Those bills can be charged to her the Probate estate (Probate Chap. VIII, Sec. 320A).

You also have rights in the probate procedure. For example, you have the right to ask the court to grant you a family allowance, that is enough money to support you and your infant son for up to a year while the estate is being probated (Probate Chap. VIII, Sec. 286 and 287)."

"Sounds good to me."

The judge did grant a family allowance to Nancy's son; and an allowance to Alan, so that he could remain home for several months to care for the child. Nancy's daughter had to share what little cash was left after the funeral expenses, and the cost of probate, with her half brother. And with a relatively young and healthy stepfather, it will probably be a long time before he dies and Nancy's daughter can take her half of the homestead.

Maybe Nancy did not change her Will because she wanted to provide for her daughter. If that was the case, then had she consulted with an attorney, he could have suggested an estate plan that would not have been challenged. But the moral of the story, for the purpose of this discussion, is that if you believe the decedent's Will is not valid, or is not drafted according to Texas law, then you need to consult with an attorney experienced in Probate matters to determine your legal rights under the Will.

Getting Possession Of The Property 6

Knowing who is entitled to receive the decedent's property is one thing. Getting that property is another. As explained in the previous chapter if the property is held jointly with rights of survivorship, or in a trust for someone, then the property belongs to the joint survivor or beneficiary and that person can get possession of the property simply by giving a certified copy of the death certificate to the financial institution.

If the decedent held property in his name only, then some sort of probate procedure is necessary in order to transfer ownership to the proper beneficiary. In Texas, most probate procedures require the assistance of an attorney, but there are a few items that you can obtain on your own. This chapter explains the various probate procedures and when it is appropriate to use that procedure.

DISTRIBUTING PERSONAL PROPERTY

Too often, the first person to discover the body will help himself to the decedent's *personal effects* (clothing, jewelry, appliances, electrical equipment, cameras, books, household items and furnishing, etc.). Unless that person is the decedent's sole beneficiary, such action is unconscionable, if not illegal.

If the decedent was married and did not have children, then all of the decedent's personal effects belong to his spouse unless he left a Will giving a particular item of personal property to someone else. If the decedent was the head of a household, then his spouse is entitled to keep all of the personal items, as described on page 85, free of any creditor claims.

If the decedent was not married, then all of his personal effects should be given to the person appointed as the Personal Representative. The Personal Representative then has the duty to distribute the property according to the decedent's Will, or if the decedent died intestate, according to the Texas Rules of Descent and Distribution.

Property located within a building is personal property. If someone inherits real property with a building or home located on that land, then the items located within the structure do not go with the gift of the land, unless the decedent left a Will saying to give that personal property to the beneficiary of that property (Probate Chap. IV, Sec. 58(c)).

If you determine that there is no need for a Probate procedure and the decedent did not have a Will then his next of kin need to divide all of the personal effects among themselves in approximately equal proportions.

WHAT'S EQUAL?

The decedent's Will or if no Will, then the Texas Rules of Descent and Distribution may direct that the decedent's personal property be divided equally between two or more beneficiaries. The problem with the term "equal" is that people have different ideas of what "equal" means. Unless there is clear evidence that the decedent's Will meant something else, "equal" refers to the monetary value of the item and not to the number of items received. For example, to divide the decedent's personal effects equally, one beneficiary may receive an expensive item of jewelry and another beneficiary may receive several items whose overall value is approximately equal to that single piece of jewelry.

When distributing personal effects there needs to be cooperation and perhaps compromise, or else bitter arguments might arise over items of little monetary value.

One such argument occurred when an elderly woman died who was rich only in her love for her five children and 12 grandchildren. After the funeral, the children gathered in their mother's rented apartment. Most of her personal effects had little, if any, monetary value. The furniture was worth less than it cost to ship.

The children decided to donate all of their mother's property to a local charity with the exception of a few items of sentimental value. Each child took some small item as a remembrance — a handkerchief, a large platter that their mother used to serve family dinners, a doily their mother crocheted.

Things went smoothly until it came to her photograph album. Frank, the youngest sibling, said, "I'll take this." Marie objected saying, "But there are pictures in that album that I want."

Frank snapped back, "You already took all the pictures Mom had on her dresser."

The argument went downhill from there. Unsettled sibling rivalries boiled over, fueled by the hurt of the loss that they were all experiencing.

It almost came to blows when the eldest settled the argument: "Frank you make copies of all of the photos in the album for Marie. Marie, you make copies of all of the pictures that you took and give them to Frank. This way you both will have a complete set of Mom's pictures.

And while you're at it, make copies for the rest of us."

IRS REFUNDS OF $500 OR LESS

As explained in Chapter 2, you need to file the decedent's final income tax return (IRS form 1040) during the tax season following the date of death. If there is a refund due to the decedent and you are entitled to that money as the beneficiary of the decedent, then you can obtain the refund by filing IRS form 1310 along with the 1040. You can obtain this form 1310 from the decedent's accountant, or if he did not have an accountant and you wish to file it yourself, then call the IRS at (800) 829-3676 to obtain the proper form. You can obtain forms, instructions, and publications from the IRS at the following Web sites:

 INTERNAL REVENUE SERVICE WEB SITE
IRS FORMS AND INSTRUCTIONS
http://www.irs.ustreas.gov/prod/forms_pubs/forms.html
IRS PUBLICATIONS
http://www.irs.ustreas.gov/prod/forms_pubs/pubs.html

If you are appointed Personal Representative as part of a probate procedure, then you do not need to file form 1310 because once you file the decedent's final income tax return, any refund will be forwarded to you as Personal Representative. Similarly, a surviving spouse does not need to file form 1310 because the spouse will automatically receive any refund due as part of their joint return.

DEPOSITING THE CHECK

If the refund check is in the name of the decedent and you have a joint account with the decedent, then you can print on the back of the check: **FOR DEPOSIT ONLY** followed by the account number, and then deposit the check to that account. If the refund check is in the name of the decedent and there is no joint account, then you may be able to obtain possession of the funds you may by using the affidavit described on page 127.

SPOUSE ➤ GETTING THE LAST PAYCHECK

If there is going to be a Probate procedure, then whoever is appointed as Personal Representative can collect (and then distribute) the decedent's paycheck as part of the settlement of the estate. If no one has been appointed as Personal Representative, then the spouse can use an *Affidavit* (a sworn written statement) to collect the decedent's last pay check, including any unpaid sick pay or vacation pay. All the spouse need do is give the Affidavit to the employer. If the employer gives the money to the spouse and it later turns out that the money should have gone to another, then, under Texas law, the employer has no liability and the spouse must make good the loss (Probate Chap.VI, Sec. 160 (b)). The following is a sample affidavit that the spouse can use:

LAST PAYCHECK AFFIDAVIT

Affiant declares that the following is true:

1.   The decedent _____
died on _____ (date). A certified copy of the death certificate is attached to this Affidavit.

2.   I am the surviving spouse of the decedent and I am entitled to the earnings under the Will or by intestate succession and no one has a superior right to the earnings.

3.   No one has qualified as executor or administrator of the decedent's estate.

4. This Affidavit is given pursuant to Probate Code Chapter VI, Section 160(b) for the purpose of collecting the decedent's last paycheck including unpaid sick pay or vacation pay.

I affirm or declare under penalty of perjury that the foregoing is true and correct.

Affiant Name and address _____

Affiant Signature _____ date_____

at _____ County, state of_____

_____

Notary Signature and Seal

TRANSFERRING PROPERTY BY AFFIDAVIT

If the decedent was unmarried, and he had property titled in his name only, or if the decedent was married and the spouse needed to get property other than the last paycheck, then Texas statute (Probate, Chap. VI, Sec. 137) allows that property to be transferred to the proper beneficiary by means of an Affidavit, provided all of the following are true:

☑ The decedent died without a Will.

☑ Everyone entitled to inherit the property signs the Affidavit.

☑ The total value of the decedent's estate (not counting the homestead and exempt property listed on page 87) is not greater than $50,000.

☑ No one has been appointed as Personal Representative and no one is in the process of having a Personal Representative appointed.

☑ At least 30 days have passed since the decedent died.

☑ The Probate court approves the Affidavit.

A sample Affidavit, and an explanation of how to complete it, follows.

SMALL ESTATE AFFIDAVIT
pursuant to Texas Probate Code Section 137

STATE OF TEXAS   )
COUNTY OF _____)

Affiant being duly sworn states:
1. We are the distributees of the estate of the decedent. Our name and address are as stated in Paragraph 10.

2. The decedent's name is _____.

3. The decedent's place of residence at the time of his death was
_____
Address   City   State   County

4. Thirty days have elapsed since the death of the decedent. A certified copy of the death certificate is attached to this Affidavit.

5. No petition for the appointment of a personal representative is pending or has been granted.

6. All of the decedent's known assets are as follows:
ASSET   LOCATION OF ASSET   VALUE OF ASSET
_____
_____

7. The value of the entire assets of the estate, not including homestead and exempt property, does not exceed $50,000.

8. All of the decedent's known liabilities are as follows:
LIABILITY   NAME AND ADDRESS OF CREDITOR
_____
_____

9. Provision for payment of these outstanding liabilities is as follows:

LIABILITY   PROVISION FOR PAYMENT
_____

SMALL ESTATE AFFIDAVIT (continued)

10. The decedent died intestate. The names, places of residence and relationships of the decedent's distributees, and the portion of the estate to which each distributee is entitled is as follows:

Name, relationship and place of residence	Age of minor	Portion of Estate

11. This Affidavit is signed by each distributee or by the natural guardian or next of kin of any minor or the guardian of any other incapacitated person who is a distributee. This Affidavit is signed by two disinterested witnesses.

The foregoing statement is made under penalty of perjury

_____
Signature of Affiant

_____
Signature of Affiant

_____
Signature of Affiant

_____
Signature of Witness

_____
Signature of Witness

Subscribed and sworn to before me this date _____

_____
Notary Public
Seal

HOW TO COMPLETE THE AFFIDAVIT

Paragraphs 1 and 10: IDENTITY OF AFFIANT

A *distributee* is a person who inherits the decedent's personal property under the Texas Rules of Descent and Distribution (see Chapter 5 for an explanation of the law). If you have any question about who has the right to inherit the estate or if you cannot find one of the distributees, then it is best to consult with an attorney before attempting to take possession of the decedent's property.

PARAGRAPH 6: THE DECEDENT'S ASSETS

You need to list all of the property owned by the decedent at the time of his death. That includes real property, and personal property he held in his name only, or jointly, or in trust for someone.

PARAGRAPH 8: IDENTITY OF CREDITORS

You need to identify all of the decedent's creditors (See Chapter 4). You need to make provision to pay any valid debt from the proceeds of the money you receive. If there are more debts than money, then consult with an attorney before using this Affidavit.

PARAGRAPH 11: SIGNING THE AFFIDAVIT

All those entitled to inherit the decedent's property must sign the Affidavit in the presence of a Notary Public and two disinterested witnesses. A *disinterested witness* is someone who has no monetary interest in the estate; i.e., they are not a creditor of the estate, nor are they a distributee of the estate. The spouse of a distributee may have an indirect interest so it is best that the spouse not serve as a witness. If one of the distributees is a child then the parent or legal guardian must sign for the child. If a distributee is too incapacitated to sign, and has no guardian, then consult with an attorney about arranging to have someone sign for that person.

CAUTION YOUR LIABILITY

If you use this Affidavit, then you become personally liable to anyone who had a right to the decedent's money. For example, if some relative was entitled to receive a share of the money, and you did not identify that person as a distributee — or if the decedent owed money on a credit card, and you neglect to pay that debt as promised in Paragraph 9 of the Affidavit. In such cases, the person who had a right to the property, can sue you personally for the amount of money you received using the Affidavit. If they win, you will need to return the money AND you may need to pay attorney's fees (Probate Chap.VI, Sec.138).

FILING THE AFFIDAVIT WITH THE COURT

Once you complete the affidavit, you need to take it to the Probate court together with the filing fee. You will need to go to the court in the county of the decedent's residence. If the decedent did not live in this state, then take the Affidavit to the county where the personal property is located. For example, if you are trying to get a bank account and the decedent lived out of state, then go to the Probate court in the county where the bank is located (Probate, Chap. I, Sec. 6 & 7).

You may save time if you first call the Probate court and ask the Clerk the following questions:

How do I get to the courthouse?
When is the best time to meet with you?
What is the current filing fee?
Do I need to pay in cash?
What documents do I need to bring with me?
How long does it take to get the Affidavit approved?

USING THE AFFIDAVIT TO GET THE PROPERTY

Once the judge is satisfied that the statute applies in your case, he will approve the Affidavit. The Clerk will prepare as many certified copies of the approved Affidavit as you request. There is a charge for each copy. You will need a copy for each company. For example, if the decedent owned a brokerage account worth $15,000 and a CD worth $10,000, then you need two copies, one for the brokerage firm and the other for the bank.

You might save time if you first call the institution and make arrangements to have the property turned over to whoever is entitled to receive it (the person(s) identified in Paragraph 10 of the Affidavit).

USING THE AFFIDAVIT TO TRANSFER THE HOMESTEAD

The Small Estate Affidavit cannot be used to transfer real property, with the exception of the decedent's homestead. You can have the homestead transferred to the proper beneficiary by giving the legal description of the homestead in Paragraph 6, and by identifying those who inherit the property in Paragraph 10. If the judge approves the Affidavit, then you need to have a certified copy of the Affidavit recorded in real property division of the county where the property is located. Once the Affidavit is recorded, the person(s) who inherit the property are free to take possession of the property and/or sell it (Probate Chap. VI, Sec. 137(c)).

You will need to go through a full Probate procedure to transfer any other parcel of real property owned by the decedent. If you need a full probate, then do not use the Affidavit because all of the decedent's probate estate will be transferred as part of that procedure. The full Probate procedure is discussed later in this chapter.

GETTING THE CONTENTS
OF THE SAFE DEPOSIT BOX

If the decedent leased a safe deposit box together with another person, each with full authority to enter the box, then the co-lessee of the box can remove all of its contents. If, however, the decedent and another, both needed to be present in order to access the box, or if the decedent was the sole lessee of a safe deposit box, then some sort of probate procedure is necessary in order to get possession of the contents of the box.

If there is a full probate procedure a Personal Representative will be appointed by the Probate court. The court will give Letters to the Personal Representative saying that the Representative has full authority to take possession of all of the probate estate assets. If the decedent had a safe deposit box, then the Personal Representative can present the Letters to the bank or safe deposit box lessor, and they will give the Representative access to the box and all of its contents.

If the decedent's property is being transferred by means of a Small Estate Affidavit, then the Affidavit can be presented to the lessor of the safe deposit box. To prepare the Affidavit you will need to identify the contents of the box. See page 70 for information about how to obtain an inventory of the contents of the safe deposit box.

TRANSFERRING THE CAR

If the decedent owned a motor vehicle then title to the car needs to be transferred to the new owner and the car registered in the state where it is going to be used. It is a good idea to limit the use of the car until it is transferred to the beneficiary. If the decedent's car is involved in an accident before the car is transferred to the new owner, then the decedent's estate may be liable for the damage. Having adequate insurance on the car may save the estate from monetary loss, but a pending lawsuit could delay the probate procedure and prevent any money from being distributed to the beneficiaries until the lawsuit is settled.

Texas law requires that the owner of a motor vehicle have Liability insurance. Before making the transfer, have the new owner show proof of insurance. After the transfer is made, contact the decedent's insurance company and arrange to have the decedent's motor vehicle policy cancelled. The company should refund any unused premium to the estate of the decedent.

WHO IS ENTITLED TO THE MOTOR VEHICLE

As explained in chapter 5, if the decedent held the car jointly with another with rights of survivorship, then the joint owner now owns the car. The surviving owner should contact the local County Tax Assessor-Collector's office and remove the decedent's name from the title.

If the decedent owned the car with another without rights of survivorship, then the decedent's share of the car goes to whomever he named in his Will. If he died without a Will, then his share goes to his next of kin as determined in the Texas Law of Descent and Distribution (see page 106).

CAR IN DECEDENT'S NAME ONLY

If the decedent had a Will and specifically named someone to inherit his motor vehicle, then that motor vehicle goes to that person, and should be transferred to the beneficiary as soon as is practicable. If the decedent did not make a specific gift of the car in his Will then the car goes to the *residuary beneficiaries* under his Will, i.e. to those people who inherit whatever is left after all gifts specified in the Will are made and all of the bills and costs of probate are paid.

If the decedent did not have a Will, and was a resident of the state of Texas then the car belongs to the decedent's heirs as determined by the Texas Rules of Descent and Distribution.

MORE THAN ONE BENEFICIARY

If there is more than one person who has the right to inherit the car, then the beneficiaries need to decide who will take title to the car. They can all be listed as co-owners but that raises liability issues, namely, if one gets in an accident, then they all could be liable. If the beneficiaries decide to have just one person take title to the car, then that person will need to compensate the other heirs for their share of the car. That raises the question of how much the car is worth. The beneficiaries will need to come to an agreement as to the value of the car.

DETERMINING THE VALUE OF THE CAR

Cars are valued in many different ways. The *collateral* value of the car is the value that banks use to evaluate the car for purposes of making a loan to the owner of the car. Because banks print these values in book form, the collateral value is also referred to as the *book value* of the car.

If you were to trade in a car for the purpose of purchasing a new car, then the car dealer will offer you the *wholesale* value of the car. Were you to purchase that same car from a car dealer, then he will price it at its *retail* or *fair market value*. Usually the retail price is highest, wholesale is lowest, and the book value somewhere in between.

You can call your local bank to get the book value of the car. It may be more difficult to obtain the wholesale value of the car because the amount of money a dealer is willing to pay for the car depends on the value of the new car that you are purchasing. You can get some idea of the car's retail value by looking at comparable used car advertisements in the local newspaper.

 You can determine both wholesale and retail values of the car by using one or more of the search engines on the Internet to find Web sites that will give both wholesale and retail car values.

LOCATE THE CERTIFICATE OF TITLE

To make the transfer you will need to turn in the certificate of title to the Texas Department of Transportation. If you cannot find the certificate of title then you will need to obtain a new one by filing out Form 34:
APPLICATION FOR CERTIFIED COPY OF TITLE.

You can obtain this form at any one of the 17 Vehicle Title and Registration Regional Offices located throughout the state, or you can get the form from your local county Tax Assessor-Collectors office. You can get the address and telephone number of these offices by calling the Texas Department of Transportation: (512) 465-7611. For the hearing impaired call TDD (512) 302-2110.

You can also get the information from the Internet:

 TEXAS DEPARTMENT OF TRANSPORTATION WEB SITE
http://www.dot.state.tx.us/

Once you obtain a copy of the certificate, you may discover that the title identifies a lienholder (lender). In such case, you need to contact the lender to obtain a copy of the promissory note and record of payments. You will not be able to transfer title to the car unless the lender gives written permission to do so.

Some lenders will allow the loan to be assigned to a beneficiary provided the beneficiary agrees, in writing, to take over the payments. That arrangement is fine, if the company allows the estate to be released from all further liability. But, most companies will insist that the estate remain liable for the balance of payment. In such cases, it is better to have the beneficiary refinance the car and have the original loan agreement satisfied by paying it in full.

If there is going to be a Probate procedure, then the Personal Representative will transfer title to the car as part of that procedure. The Letters issued by the court will give the Representative authority to transfer title to the proper heir. If no probate procedure is necessary, then you can transfer title by using an Affidavit provided by the Texas Department of Transportation Form VTR-262: AFFIDAVIT OF HEIRSHIP FOR A MOTOR VEHICLE. You can get this form by calling the telephone number given on the previous page.

Once the transfer takes place you should notify the Department of Transportation of the change in ownership so that the decedent's estate will no longer be liable for tickets or accidents. This is done by filing Form VTR-346: MOTOR VEHICLE TRANSFER NOTIFICATION or you can write a letter to: Texas Department of Transportation
                    Customer Information Service Branch
                    Austin, Texas   78779-0001
Before writing, call them at the number given on the previous page to find out what information they require, and their service fee (currently $5).

TRANSFERRING THE MOBILE HOME

To transfer title to a mobile home, you will need to contact the Texas Department of Housing and Community Affairs. Their telephone number is (800) 500-7074. Before transferring the mobile home, you need to determine whether the land on which the mobile home is located was leased or owned by the decedent. If the decedent was renting space in a trailer park, then contact the trailer park owner to transfer the rental agreement to the beneficiary of the mobile home. If the decedent owned the land under the mobile home, then a probate procedure will be necessary to transfer the land to the proper beneficiary (see page 141).

The leased car is a not an asset of the estate because the decedent did not own the car. The leased car is a liability to the estate because the decedent was obligated to pay the balance of the monies owed on the lease agreement. The Personal Representative, or next of kin, needs to arrange to pay for the balance of payments under the lease agreement.

TERMINATING THE ESTATE'S LIABILITY

If the remaining payments exceed the current market value of the car, there may be a temptation to hand the keys over to the leasing company. This may not be the best strategy, because the leasing company can sell the car, and then sue the estate for the balance of the monies owed. If the decedent had no assets or if the only assets he had are creditor proof, then simply returning the car may be an option. But if the decedent's estate has assets available to pay the balance of the lease payments, then the Personal Representative needs to arrange to have the car transferred in a way that releases the estate from all further liability.

LITTLE OR NO ADMINISTRATION

There needs to be a probate procedure if the decedent left a Will or if there is some real property to be transferred other than the homestead. But suppose there is little or no money in the decedent's estate. In such case, the court may allow an abridged probate procedure:

NO ADMINISTRATION

If the decedent is survived by a spouse and/or minor child and the amount in the estate (not counting the homestead or exempt assets) is less than the amount that the spouse and/or minor child are entitled to as a family allowance, then no Personal Representative need be appointed. The attorney for the spouse (or minor child) can ask the court to have the family allowance distributed and order that no other administration is necessary. The Probate judge will hold a hearing and if he finds that the decedent's funeral expenses and costs of his last illness and the cost of the court procedure have been paid; and there are no funds available other than that for the family allowance, then the court will order that no administration is required and that all of the estate be given to the spouse and/or minor child (Probate, Chap. VI, Sec. 139 and 140).

SUMMARY PROCEDURE

If a Personal Representative has been appointed, and it is determined that there is not enough money to pay more than the first four classes of creditors (see Page 91), then the attorney for the Personal Representative can ask that the monies be used to pay the claims in the order provided by law, and then close out the estate. The court will hold a hearing to decide what bills are to be paid. Once the bills are paid, the court will discharge the Personal Representative and close the administration. This type of Probate procedure is called a *Summary Procedure* (Probate, Chap. VI, Sec. 143).

THE FULL PROBATE PROCEDURE

If the decedent left real property some document needs to be recorded that identities the beneficiary who is now the owner of the property. As explained, if the decedent's estate is worth $50,000 or less, then the homestead can be transferred by means of a Small Estate Affidavit. For all other transfers of real property of property, there needs to be a full probate procedure. The Personal Representative will transfer the real property to the proper beneficiary as part of that probate procedure. With or without real property, if the decedent had more than $50,000 (not counting exempt property and the homestead), then there needs to be a full procedure, unless, of course, the assets pass by rights of survivorship or are held in trust.

It is the Personal Representative's job to use the Probate Estate to pay all valid claims and then distribute what is left to the proper beneficiary. All of the decedent's debts are paid from the Probate Estate and not from Personal Representative's pocket; but if the Representative makes a mistake then he may be responsible to pay for that mistake. For example, if the Personal Representative pays a debt that did not need to be paid — or if the Personal Representative transfers property to the beneficiaries too quickly and there were still taxes due on the estate, then he may be responsible to pay for such error.

The Personal Representative needs to employ an attorney to guide him through the process. It then becomes the job of the attorney for the Personal Representative to see to it that the estate is administered properly and without any personal liability to the Representative. The attorney has the right to charge reasonable fees and to charge those fees to the decedent's Estate.

APPOINTING THE REPRESENTATIVE

The first step in the Probate procedure is to have someone appointed by the court as the Personal Representative. If there is a Will, the court will appoint the person named as Executor of the Will. If the decedent died intestate, then anyone with priority can file a *petition* (a request to the court) to be appointed, or have someone of their choice appointed, as the Representative (see page 27). If someone has the same or a higher priority, then the person seeking the appointment must mail a copy of the petition to each such person. Anyone with the same or a higher priority then has the right to challenge or accept the appointment (Probate Chap. VII, Sec. 179).

INDEPENDENT ADMINISTRATION

Texas law is designed to speed administration and reduce costs by allowing the Personal Representative the right to act independently and without court supervision. This is called an *Independent Administration*. The court will allow an Independent Administration if the decedent's Will asks that the only action the court is to take is to:
☑ determine whether the Will is valid
☑ require the Personal Representative to file the inventory
☑ require the Personal Representative to file a list of claims filed against the estate.

If the Will does not require an Independent Administration (or if the decedent died without a Will) the court can allow an Independent Administration if all of the beneficiaries of the estate request it (Probate, Chap VI, Sec. 145).

CAUTION — FOR BENEFICIARY WHO IS NOT PERSONAL REPRESENTATIVE

Allowing the Representative to act independently can save the estate money, but the downside is that without court supervision the Personal Representative can do some serious mischief. With Independent Administration, the Personal Representative can do all of the following without asking your permission, or the court's permission to do so:

⇨ take possession of all of the estate assets

⇨ distribute exempt property and the family allowance

⇨ continue the decedent's business

⇨ settle claims against the decedent's estate

⇨ employ accountants, appraisers, attorneys

⇨ invest money of the estate.

(Probate Chap. VI, Sec. 146 and Chap. VII, Sec. 232, 234)

Before the court allows an Independent Administration that is not requested in the Will, all beneficiaries of the estate must be notified that the Personal Representative has applied to act independently. If you are concerned about the ability of the Personal Representative to properly administer the estate, then do not hesitate to object and request a Supervised Administration. The court will hold a hearing on the matter and rule on your request (Probate Chap VI, Sec. 145).

If the court denies your request for a supervised administration, then you can always ask the court to require the Personal Representative to provide a bond that will reimburse you for any loss you may suffer, in case the Representative does not perform his duties according to Texas law (Probate Chap. VII, Sec.194).

YOUR RIGHTS AS A BENEFICIARY

If you are the beneficiary of an estate, then you have many rights. First and foremost, you have the right to be kept informed as to the progress of the Probate procedure. At any time during the Probate, you can file a written request to have the Clerk mail you a copy of any document that is filed as part of the Probate. There is a charge for the service, so you need to ask the Clerk the cost of obtaining the copies (Probate Chap. I, 33(j)).

✧ RIGHT TO YOUR OWN ATTORNEY

The attorney who handles the estate is employed by, and represents, the Personal Representative. If the estate is sizeable, then you might consider employing your own attorney to check that things are done properly and in a timely manner.

✧ RIGHT TO A COPY OF THE WILL

If there is a Will then you have the right to receive a copy of that Will. As soon as the Personal Representative is appointed have him, or his attorney, mail you a copy. You can also get one from the court clerk.

✧ RIGHT TO COPY OF INVENTORY

Whether or not the Administration is being supervised by the court, the Personal Representative must file an inventory of all the assets of the Probate estate. You have the right to ask the Personal Representative, or his attorney to provide you with a copy of the inventory as soon as it is filed with the court. If you wish, you can ask the court clerk to provide you with a copy.

✧   RIGHT TO DEMAND SUFFICIENT BOND

It doesn't happen often, but every now and again a Personal Representative will run off with estate funds. A bond is insurance for the estate. If estate monies are stolen then the company that issued the bond will reimburse the estate for the loss. You, as a beneficiary, have the right to ask that the Personal Representative be bonded and the amount of the bond be sufficient to protect all of the estate funds. If it happens that the decedent left a Will requesting that no bond be required, then the Court will not order one unless you can prove to the Court that the Representative is mismanaging the estate property.

If the Court has ordered that the Personal Representative be bonded, then once you have a copy of the inventory and know the value of the estate, compare it to the value of the bond posted by the Representative. If the bond is less than the value of the estate, then you can ask the court to have the bond increased. Before making the request, consider that the cost of the bond is paid by the estate. If the administration of the estate is such that the decedent's real property cannot be transferred without a court order, then it may be sufficient just to cover the liquid assets of the estate. (Probate Chap. VI, Sec. 149 and Sec. 170).

✧ RIGHT TO AN ACCOUNTING

Anytime after 15 months from the date that the Independent Administration was created, you can demand that the Personal Representative give you a complete accounting stating exactly what estate property came into his hands and what he did with it. As part of the accounting ask that you be given copies of all tax returns that the Personal Representative has filed. If the Personal Representative fails to file a return, or fails to pay taxes, or if he under-reports a tax obligation, then you could later be called on to pay estate taxes out of the proceeds that you receive. If the Representative fails to make the accounting, or if you discover that the estate is being grossly mismanaged, then you have the right to ask the court that he be removed and another Personal Representative appointed (Probate, Chap. VI, Sec. 149 B & C).

✧ RIGHT TO KNOW WHAT FEES ARE CHARGED

You have the right to know how much the estate will be charged for Personal Representative and attorney fees. The Personal Representative is entitled take a commission of 5% of all sums he actually receives in cash and 5% of the money he pays out in cash, but he may not charge a fee greater than 5% of the gross fair market value of the probate estate (Probate Chap. VII, Sec. 241).

If the Personal Representative is also a beneficiary of the estate he may decide not to take a fee and just take his inheritance. The reason may be economic. Any fee he takes is taxable as ordinary income, but monies inherited are not taxable to him as a beneficiary. Ask the Representative to tell you, in writing, whether he intends to charge a fee, and if so, how much. Also ask how much he expects to pay in attorney's fees.

✧ RIGHT TO YOUR SHARE OF THE ESTATE

The Probate procedure can take anywhere from a few months to more than a year depending on the size and complexity of the Probate Estate. Unless there is a major problem with a Probate procedure, it should not take more than a year to settle the estate and get your inheritance to you. If there is an Independent Administration and two years have passed, then you have the right to ask the court to take charge of the estate, get an accounting and order that the distribution of the estate to the beneficiaries (Probate Chap. VI, Sec. 149(B)).

✧ IT'S YOUR RIGHT - DON'T BE INTIMIDATED

You may feel uncomfortable being assertive with a friend or family member who is Personal Representative. Don't be. It's your money and your legal right to be kept informed. Be especially firm if the Representative waives you off with:

"You've known me for years. Surely you trust me."

People who are trustworthy, don't ask to be trusted. They do what is right. The very fact that the Personal Representative is resisting, is a red flag. In such case, you can explain that it is not a matter of trust, but a matter of what is your legal right.

At the same time, keep things in perspective. Your family relationship may be more important, than the money you inherit. The job of Personal Representative is often complex and demanding. If the Personal Representative is getting the job done, then let him know that you appreciate his efforts.

THE CHECK LIST

We have discussed many things that need to be done when someone dies in the state of Texas. There is a check list on the opposite page that you may find helpful.

You can check those items that you need to do, and then cross them off the list once they are done. We made the list as comprehensive as possible, so many items may not apply in your case. In such case, you can cross them off the list or mark them *N/A* (not applicable).

Things to do

FUNERAL ARRANGEMENTS TO BE MADE
☐ AUTOPSY   ☐ ANATOMICAL GIFT
☐ DISPOSITION OF BODY OR ASHES

DEATH CERTIFICATE
☐ SET ASIDE A COPY FOR EACH PARCEL OF LAND
GIVE COPY TO: _____

_____

NOTICE OF DEATH
PEOPLE TO BE NOTIFIED _____

COMPANIES TO NOTIFY
☐ TELEPHONE COMPANY
    ☐ LOCAL CARRIER   ☐ LONG DISTANCE   ☐ CELLULAR
☐ NEWSPAPER (OBITUARY PRINTED)
☐ NEWSPAPER CANCELLED   ☐ deposit refund
☐ SOCIAL SECURITY
☐ INTERNET SERVER
☐ TELEVISION CABLE COMPANY
☐ BASE POWER & LIGHT   ☐ deposit refund
☐ POST OFFICE
☐ OTHER UTILITIES (GAS, WATER)   ☐ deposit refund
☐ PENSION PLAN
☐ ANNUITY
☐ HEALTH INSURANCE COMPANY
☐ LIFE INSURANCE COMPANY
☐ HOME INSURANCE COMPANY
☐ MOTOR VEHICLE INSURANCE COMPANY
☐ CONDOMINIUM OR HOMEOWNER ASSOCIATION
☐ CANCEL SERVICE CONTRACT   ☐ deposit refund
☐ CREDIT CARD COMPANIES _____

    _____

    _____

Things to do

REMOVE DECEDENT AS BENEFICIARY OF:
- ☐ WILL ☐ INSURANCE POLICY ☐ PENSION PLAN
- ☐ BANK OR IRA ACCOUNT ☐ SECURITY

DEBTS

PAY DECEDENT'S DEBTS (AMOUNT & CREDITOR)

_____

COLLECT MONIES OWED TO DECEDENT (AMOUNT & DEBTOR)

_____

TAXES
- ☐ FILE FINAL FEDERAL INCOME TAX RETURN
- ☐ FILE FINAL STATE INCOME TAX RETURN
- ☐ RECEIVE INCOME TAX REFUND
- ☐ FILE ESTATE TAX RETURN

PROPERTY TO BE TRANSFERRED
- ☐ PERSONAL EFFECTS
- ☐ MOTOR VEHICLE
- ☐ BANK ACCOUNT
- ☐ CREDIT UNION ACCOUNT
- ☐ IRA ACCOUNT
- ☐ SECURITIES
- ☐ BROKERAGE ACCOUNT
- ☐ INSURANCE PROCEEDS
- ☐ HOMESTEAD
- ☐ TIME SHARE
- ☐ OTHER REAL PROPERTY
- ☐ CONTENTS OF SAFE DEPOSIT BOX

OTHER THINGS TO DO

_____

_____

_____

Things to do

FUNERAL ARRANGEMENTS TO BE MADE
☐ AUTOPSY ☐ ANATOMICAL GIFT
☐ DISPOSITION OF BODY OR ASHES

DEATH CERTIFICATE
☐ SET ASIDE A COPY FOR EACH PARCEL OF LAND
GIVE COPY TO: _____
_____

NOTICE OF DEATH
PEOPLE TO BE NOTIFIED _____

COMPANIES TO NOTIFY
☐ TELEPHONE COMPANY
   ☐ LOCAL CARRIER ☐ LONG DISTANCE ☐ CELLULAR
☐ NEWSPAPER (OBITUARY PRINTED)
☐ NEWSPAPER CANCELLED   ☐ deposit refund
☐ SOCIAL SECURITY
☐ INTERNET SERVER
☐ TELEVISION CABLE COMPANY
☐ BASE POWER & LIGHT   ☐ deposit refund
☐ POST OFFICE
☐ OTHER UTILITIES (GAS, WATER)   ☐ deposit refund
☐ PENSION PLAN
☐ ANNUITY
☐ HEALTH INSURANCE COMPANY
☐ LIFE INSURANCE COMPANY
☐ HOME INSURANCE COMPANY
☐ MOTOR VEHICLE INSURANCE COMPANY
☐ CONDOMINIUM OR HOMEOWNER ASSOCIATION
☐ CANCEL SERVICE CONTRACT   ☐ deposit refund
☐ CREDIT CARD COMPANIES _____

_____
_____

Preneed Arrangements 7

Death is a wake-up call because once someone close to us dies we are reminded of our own mortality. We realize that death can be put off, but the inevitable is inevitable. Although we cannot change the fact of our death, we have the power to control the circumstances of our death by making preneed arrangements.

You can make preneed arrangements so that you will be buried in the manner you wish and where you wish. You can also make arrangements that direct the kind of medical treatments you want to be given in the event you become seriously ill.

You can legally appoint someone to make your medical decisions in the event that you are too ill to speak for yourself. If you let that person know how you feel about life support systems, autopsies and anatomical gifts then that person will be authorized to act on your behalf and will see to it that your wishes are carried out.

As this chapter will show, it is relatively simple and inexpensive to make such preneed arrangements.

MAKING BURIAL ARRANGEMENTS

When making burial arrangements for the decedent, you may decide to purchase one or more burial spaces nearby for yourself or other family members.

If the decedent was buried in the family plot, then this is the time to take inventory of the number of spaces left and who in the family expects to use those spaces.

If all of the spaces are taken and if you plan to be cremated, then as explained in Chapter 1, some cemeteries will allow an urn to be placed in an occupied family plot. You can call the cemetery and ask them to explain their policy as it relates to the burial of an urn in a currently occupied grave site or mausoleum.

If this is not an option, and the cemetery of your choice has a columbarium, you might consider purchasing a space at this time.

If you wish to have your cremains scattered, then you need to let your next of kin know where and how this is to be done.

VETERAN OR
VETERAN'S SPOUSE

If you are an honorably discharged veteran, you have the right to be buried in a Veterans National Cemetery. You cannot reserve a grave site in advance. If your Veteran spouse was buried in a Veterans National Cemetery then you have the right to be buried in that same grave site unless soil conditions require a separate grave site.

If you wish to be buried in a Veterans National Cemetery, then check on current availability (see page 14 for telephone numbers). Let your next of kin know your choice of cemetery.

To establish your eligibility your next of kin will need to provide the following information:

➤ the veteran's rank, serial, social security and VA claim numbers

➤ the branch of service; the date and place of entry into and separation from the service

The next of kin will also need to provide the VA with a copy of the veteran's official military discharge document bearing an official seal or a DD 214 form.

If you wish to be buried in a national cemetery, then make all of these items readily accessible to your family.

MAKING FUNERAL ARRANGEMENTS

If you are financially able, in addition to purchasing a burial space, consider purchasing a Preneed funeral plan. It will be easier on your family emotionally and financially if you make your own funeral arrangements. If you do not have sufficient cash on hand for the kind of funeral you desire, then many funeral directors offer an installment payment plan.

Once you decide on a plan, the funeral director will present you with a Prepaid Funeral Benefits Contract. The contract may be lengthy, but it is worth your effort to take the time to read it before you sign it. If the contract is written in "legalese" then either consult with your attorney before signing it or ask as many questions of the funeral director as is necessary to make the terms of the contract clear to you.

If you are not satisfied with the way a certain section of the contract is written then add an addendum to the contract that explains, in plain English, your understanding of that passage. If you are concerned about something that is not mentioned in the contract, then insist that the contract be amended to include that item.

In particular, check to see whether the contract answers the following questions.

Does the contract cover all costs?

The contract should contain an itemized list stating exactly what goods and services are included in the sales price. Ask the funeral director whether there will be any additional cost when you die. If you have not made provision for a burial space, then you may want to arrange for a burial space at this time. If you have made provision for a burial space, then you need to make the funeral director aware of the arrangement (Finance 154.151(b)(3)).

Is the price guaranteed?

Some preneed plans have a fixed price for the goods and services you chose. You are guaranteed that the goods and services will be provided upon your death, regardless of when you finally die. Other contracts do not guarantee that the price will be the same. The price for the goods and services that you have chosen under those contracts are not fixed, and the company can charge additional monies upon your death. You need to check the contract to see which is the case under the plan that you are purchasing.

How are your contract funds protected?

Texas laws are designed to protect the purchaser of Prepaid Funeral Benefits. According to Texas law, funeral firms are required to protect funds paid by the consumer by placing the monies into a trust, or by having the funeral firm purchase a life insurance policy or an annuity to cover the funds paid by the purchaser (Finance 154.201, 154.253).

Check to see if your Prepaid Funeral Benefits contract states how your monies will be protected. If the contract is silent on the issue, then have the funeral director explain how the funeral firm will guarantee your plan. If the funds are protected by being placed in a trust account, then the funeral firm must deposit your payment funds within 30 days. Similarly, if the funds are protected by insurance, then the funeral firm must submit the premium within 30 days (Finance 154.203(a) and 154.253(a)).

If the funds are to be deposited into a trust, then have the funeral firm agree to furnish you with proof of deposit. Have the funeral firm promise, in writing, to notify you should they decide to change banks. If the funds are protected with by an insurance policy, then have them furnish you with proof of payment of the premium.

Is the funeral firm reputable?

Of course all of these safeguards may fail if you are not doing business with a reputable funeral firm. It is prudent to take the time to call the investigation division of the Texas Funeral Service Commission at (512) 470-7222 or toll free (888) 667-4881. Ask them if the funeral firm is licensed and whether any complaints have been filed against them.

Can you cancel the contract?

Texas law provides that you have the right to cancel the contract and receive your money back. The only question is how much of your money is the funeral firm required to return to you. Texas law recognizes that the funeral firm is entitled to recover monies they spent setting up the contract, so if you cancel the contract during the first year the law allows them to keep up to 10% of the monies you paid. If you put less than 10% of the contract price down, and cancel the contract the seller is entitled to keep up to half of what you paid (Finance, 154.155, 154.252, 154.254).

If your prepaid funeral contract is funded by an insurance policy, then if you cancel the contract within the first year you are entitled to the cash surrender value of the policy (Finance 154.205). That amount could be significantly less than you paid. If you paid several thousand dollars for the funeral plan then it could cost you several hundred dollars to cancel the contract. It is important that you know exactly how much money you will get back if you later decided to cancel the contract.

People who are applying for, or receiving, Medicaid, Supplemental Security Income ("SSI") or other public assistance program have limits on the amount of assets that they can own. If an applicant for any of these programs purchases a Prepaid Funeral plan and signs a *waiver* giving up their right to cancel the contract, then the purchase will not affect their eligibility to qualify for the program. If you purchase a contract and then later need to apply for any of these programs you can have the funeral firm change the contract to one that is irrevocable by signing the waiver (Finance 154.156).

What if you die in another state or country?
It is a good idea to have the contract spell out what provision will be made in the event that you move to another state or in the event you happen to die in another state or country. Many funeral firms are part of a national funeral service corporation with funeral firms located throughout the United States, so this is not usually a problem.

Can the plan be changed?
Texas statue states that you can cancel your contract and receive your money back, but suppose your heirs need to change the plan you have chosen because:
➤ your body is missing or cannot be recovered
➤ you were buried by another facility because your heirs were unaware of your Prepaid contract
➤ you died in another country and were buried there.

But what if your heirs decide on a plan different than the one you purchased? Funeral firms generally allow heirs to make changes to the plan you paid for such as:
➤ purchasing a more expensive plan and paying for the difference
➤ changing to a lesser plan and receiving a refund.
You need to check whether the contract offered by the funeral firm addresses the issue of making changes to the contract after your death.

You may wonder why anyone would think of changing the decedent's funeral plan, but consider that in today's market, it is not uncommon for a Prepaid Funeral Benefits contract to cost several thousand dollars. A top end funeral complete with solid bronze casket can cost upwards of $40,000.

And there may be other motivations. Consider the case of Mona, a difficult woman with a personality that can only be described as "sour." Her husband deserted her after four years of marriage leaving her to raise their son, Lester, by herself. Once Lester was grown, Mona made it clear to him that she had done her job and now he was on his own.

Lester could have used some help. He married and had three children. One of his children suffered with asthma and it was a constant struggle to keep up with the medical bills.

Mona believed in being good to herself. She did not intend to, nor did she, leave much money when she died. She knew that Lester would not be able to afford a "proper" burial for her, so she purchased a funeral plan and paid more than $15,000 for it. She was pleased when the funeral director told her that the monies would be kept in trust in a local bank until the time they were needed.

Lester was not familiar with Texas law, so when Mona died he asked an attorney at the Legal Aid office to determine whether the Prepaid Funeral Benefits contract was revocable.

It was.

You know the ending to this story.

PURCHASING BURIAL INSURANCE

If you are concerned that you get the exact type of funeral that you want, with no changes, then you can purchase a Prepaid Funeral Benefits contract; use the insurance method of protecting your funds and then irrevocably assign your ownership of the rights to the benefits under the insurance policy to the funeral provider (Finance 154.206).

If you want to make provision to pay for your funeral and want to give your family flexibility in choice of funeral plan, then consider purchasing a life insurance policy payable to whoever has the responsibility of seeing to your burial. The cost of the policy might be less than purchasing a Prepaid Funeral Benefit contract. You could insure yourself with enough money to cover the cost of the burial and other miscellaneous expenses such as paying for a dinner after the burial, or paying the airfare for a family member to attend the service.

If you name a family member as the beneficiary of the policy, then it is important that the family member clearly understands why he/she is named as beneficiary. It is equally important that the beneficiary agree to use the monies for the intended purpose. It isn't so much that a family member is not trustworthy as it is that they may not understand what you intended — especially in those cases where other funds are available to pay for the funeral. Too often insurance funds are left to a son or daughter who then refuses to contribute to the cost of the funeral saying in effect "Dad wanted me to have this money — that's why he left it to me."

To avoid a misunderstanding, put it in writing. It need not be a formal contract. It could be something as simple as a letter to the insurance beneficiary, with copies to your next of kin, saying something like:

Dear Romita,

I purchased a $10,000 insurance policy today naming you as beneficiary of the policy. As we discussed this money is to be used to pay for the following:

- my funeral and grave site
- my headstone
- perpetual care for my grave
- airfare for each of my grandchildren to attend the funeral
- dinner for the family after the wake
- lunch for the family after the funeral

If there is any money left over, please accept it as my thanks for all the effort spent on my behalf.

Love,
Dad

P.S. I am sending a copy of this letter to your brother so that he will know that all arrangements have been made.

Whether or not you arrange to pay for your burial or funeral, you need to let your next of kin know your feelings about the burial procedure. Let your family know whether you wish to be cremated or buried. If you wish to have a religious service, then let your family know the type of service and where it is to be held. Let the family know where you wish to be buried, or if you intend to be cremated, then where to place the ashes.

AUTOPSIES

As discussed in Chapter 1, some autopsies are optional. If you have strong feelings about allowing an optional autopsy or not allowing the procedure, then let your family know how you feel.

ANATOMICAL GIFTS

If you wish to make an anatomical gift, you can make that donation by completing a donor card or by letting your family know that you wish to make a donation of some or all of your body parts. Donor cards are available at your local Driver's License Facility.

If you are aged, and in poor health, the local Organ Procurement Organization will probably not consider your body for transplantation of body parts, but you can still donate your body for education and research. If you wish to make such as donation, call or write to either University mentioned on page 6. They will forward a Dedication Form to you along with information on the subject. As discussed in Chapter 1, there may be a significant charge to your   estate to make the donation, so you need to be aware of the cost before you decide to make the gift.

PREPARING A HEALTH CARE DIRECTIVE

If you do not wish to make an anatomical gift, then let your family know how you feel. Of course, there are problems with just telling someone how you feel about your burial arrangements, autopsies, and anatomical gifts:

YOU TELL THE WRONG PERSON

The person you confide in may not be present when the arrangements are made. For example, if you tell your spouse what arrangements to make then he/she may die before you do — or you could die simultaneously in a car or plane crash.

You may tell someone who does not have authority to carry out your wishes. That was the case with James. After his wife died, he moved to a retirement community where he lived for 8 years until his death. James had two sons who lived in different states. Although he loved his sons, he had difficulty talking to either of them about serious matters. It was easier for him to talk with his friends in the retirement community. They often spoke about dying and how they felt about different burial arrangements. James would reminisce about his youth and growing up in a farming community in the plains state of Kansas. "I was happy and free. Out there you had room to breathe. It would be nice to be buried there — peaceful and spacious."

When he died, his friends told his sons about their father's desire to be buried in Kansas. They met the suggestion with scepticism and pragmatism:
"Dad didn't say anything like that to me."
"It would cost us double, if we had to arrange for burial in another state. I'm sure he didn't have that kind of expense in mind."

THE PERSON DOES NOT CARRY OUT YOUR WISHES

The person you tell may not understand what you said or perhaps they hear only what they want to hear. An example that comes to mind is the mother who constantly complained that she felt like a burden to her children. She would often say "When I die, burn my body and throw my ashes out to sea." Her children paid no attention. When she died she was given a full funeral and buried in a local cemetery. They never asked, nor did they consider, that their mother might really have wanted to be cremated.

WHO WANTS TO TALK ABOUT IT?

For many people the main problem with telling someone what to do when you die is talking about your death. It may be an uncomfortable, if not unpleasant, subject for you to bring up, and for your family to discuss. If this is the case, then consider putting the information in writing and give the instructions to the person who will have the job of carrying out your wishes.

You can legally appoint someone to carry out your wishes relating to the care of your person, by signing a document called a *Medical Power of Attorney*. Texas statute contains a statutory form that you can use to appoint a Health Care Agent to carry out the wishes you express in the Medical Power of Attorney. You can look up the statutory form of the Medical Power of Attorney (Health & Safety 166.163, 166.164) by going to the nearest public library or courthouse library. You can also download the form from the internet:

TEXAS STATUTES
http://capitol.tlc.state.tx.us/statutes/statutes.html

DIRECTIVE TO PHYSICIANS

In addition to appointing someone to make your medical decisions, it is important to give that person directions about the kind of care you want in the event that you are too ill to make your own health care decisions. Tell your Health Care Agent how you feel about having a feeding tube inserted if you could not swallow. Tell your Agent whether you want to be attached to a ventilator should you be unable to breathe on your own. Better yet, put it in writing. A *Directive to Physicians and Family or Surrogates* (the "Directive") is a statement that you do (or do not) wish life support systems to be used in the event that you are dying and there is no hope for your recovery. In many states this document is called a *Living Will*.

The Texas Advance Directives Act contains a statutory form of the Directive (Health & Safety 166.033). You can use this form to instruct your Health Care Agent what kind of treatment you wish in the event that you are too ill to speak for your self. If you have not appointed a Health Care Agent and did not sign a Directive, then your doctor will consult with your legal guardian to determine whether to continue (or discontinue) life support systems. If no legal guardian has been appointed, then Texas statute gives the following people priority to make health care decisions for you: 1st   Spouse
2nd   Your adult children
3rd   Your parents
4th   Your nearest living relative.

A person with priority must be reasonably available, willing and competent to act. If not, the next one with priority will make the decision. Whoever makes the decision must base the decision on their knowledge of what you want (Health & Safety 166.039).

If the order of priority as mandated by Texas law is not as you wish, or if there is someone you wish to exclude altogether from making your health care decisions, then it is important to sign a Medical Power of Attorney and appoint the person of your choice to act as your Health Care Agent. If not, life decisions made for you, may not be as you would have wished.

George is a case in point. His wife became ill with Alzheimer's disease. He cared for her at home for as long as he was able, but finally, it was too much for him. He placed her in a local nursing facility. He and his two daughters visited her frequently, even though she scarcely recognized them.

George and Emily met at the nursing home. Emily's husband also suffered from Alzheimer's disease and was at the same facility. After visiting with their respective spouses they would go to the local coffee shop. One thing led to another, and soon they were an item. George's daughters were not happy with the coupling. They criticized everything about Emily, from the way she dressed to her table manners.

When Emily moved in with George, his daughters made cutting remarks about Emily's moral character. Emily didn't take it personally. She believed the girls were more concerned about their inheritance than George's happiness. A second marriage might cut into what they already considered to be rightfully theirs.

Not that George and Emily planned to wed. They both loved their respective spouses and had no intention of trying to obtain a divorce. Their understanding was that if and when they both were single, they would discuss marriage at that time.

George and Emily enjoyed each other, feeling and acting like a couple of teenagers; but their happiness was short-lived. George suffered a stroke while driving a car. His injuries from the accident combined with the severity of the stroke made for a bleak prognosis. The doctors said George would die unless they put him on a ventilator and inserted a feeding tube. Even with these life support systems, they doubted that he would ever come out of the coma.

Emily pleaded to keep him alive. "Let's try everything. If he doesn't improve we can always discontinue the life support systems later."

George's daughters did not see it that way.
"Why torture him with needles and tubes? Let him pass on peacefully."

George never signed a Directive so his physicians did not know whether he wanted to be connected to a life support systems. He never appointed anyone to be his Health Care Agent to make his medical decisions in the event he was unable to do so. In the absence of a Medical Power of Attorney or a Directive instructing his physicians to apply life support systems, the doctors had no choice. Under Texas law, the daughters were 2nd in priority. Emily had no standing at all.

George died.

Everyman's Estate Plan

The first six chapters of this book describe how to wind up the affairs of the decedent. As you read those chapters, you learned about the kinds of problems that can occur when someone dies. It is relatively simple for you to make an estate plan so that your family members are not burdened with similar problems. An *estate plan* is the arranging of one's finances to reduce (if not eliminate) probate costs and estate taxes, so that your beneficiaries inherit your property quickly and at little cost.

If you think that only wealthy people need to prepare an estate plan, you are mistaken. Each year, heirs of relatively modest estates, spend thousands of dollars to settle an estate. A bit of planning could have eliminated most, if not all, of the hassle and cost suffered by those families.

The suggestions in this chapter are designed to assist the average person in preparing a practical and inexpensive estate plan, so we have named this chapter EVERYMAN'S ESTATE PLAN. Once you create your own estate plan, you can rest assured that your family will not be left with more problems than happy memories of you.

AVOIDING PROBATE

Probate procedures can be costly and time consuming. If you have a small estate and only one or two beneficiaries, then it is not all that difficult to arrange your finances so that there will be no need for probate when you die.

BANK ACCOUNTS

You can arrange to have all of your bank accounts, including certificates of deposit, titled so that the money goes directly to your heirs when you die. For example, suppose all you have is a bank account with a balance of $50,000 and you want to have this go to your son and daughter when you die.   You might think that a simple solution is to put each child's name on the account, but first consider the ramifications of a joint account:

THE JOINT ACCOUNT
A joint bank account gives each joint owner of the account complete access to that account. If you hold the account jointly with your children, then each child can write a check on that account, the same as yourself. When you die the remaining joint owner (or joint owners) can withdraw all of the money from the account. There are some potential problems with this arrangement:

⊠ POTENTIAL LIABILITY

If you hold property jointly with one of your adult children and that child is sued or gets a divorce then the child may need to disclose their ownership of the joint account. In such a case, you may find yourself spending money to prove that all of the money in that account really belongs to you.

⊠ OVERREACHING

If you set up a joint account with your child so that the child has authority to withdraw funds from the account, then funds may be withdrawn without your authorization. If you open a joint account with two of your children, then after your death the first child to the bank may decide to withdraw all of the money and that will, at the very least, cause hard feelings between them.

⊠ THE MINOR CHILD

Texas law allows a minor to own a savings or checking account either in their own name or jointly with another (Finance 34.305, 65.101, 65.102). But if you elect a minor as the joint owner of your account, would you want the child to have the ability to remove money from your account? If you die, would you want the minor to be able to go to the bank and withdraw all of the money?

Because of these inherent problems, you might want to hold the funds so that your beneficiary does not gain access to the monies until and unless you die. There are three ways to do so: the "convenience" account, the "in trust for" and the "pay-on-death" account.

THE CONVENIENCE ACCOUNT

You could set up a convenience account so that your child is available to write checks for you on the account in the event of your disability. Unless you say so, your child will have no right to any part of the account, once you die. If you make the child the beneficiary of the account, then the child will not own the account until you die (Probate, Chap. XI, 438A). This solves the liability problem in the event the child is sued, but not the problem of over-reaching. To solve the problem of overreaching, you can set up an "in trust for" ("ITF") account or a "pay on death" ("POD") account.

THE "IN TRUST FOR" ACCOUNT

You can direct a financial institution to hold your account *in trust for* one or more beneficiaries that you name. The beneficiary does not have access to that account during your lifetime. Once you die, all the beneficiary need do is present your death certificate to the bank and the funds will be given to that beneficiary.

The ITF account is very flexible. If you are married, you can make the account so that you and your spouse hold the account jointly with rights of survivorship, and in trust for one or more beneficiaries, for example:
ALBERT STASIO AND AUDREY STASIO, jointly with rights of survivorship, in trust for JOANNE STASIO and ROBERT STASIO.

Once Albert and Audrey are deceased, the monies will go to Joanne and Robert. In the event that one of the beneficiaries dies before that time, then the remaining beneficiary will receive all the monies in the account (Probate Chap. XI, Sec. 439 (c)).

THE "PAY ON DEATH" ACCOUNT

The "Pay On Death" account is much like the "in trust for" account. Instead of saying:

"I hold this account in trust for ____,"

the account holder is saying:

"When I die pay this money to _____."

As with the "in trust for" account, the "pay on death" account can be held jointly, with or without rights of survivorship.

With both the ITF and POD account:

⇨ The beneficiary does not have access to the account until the owner of the account dies.

⇨ During his lifetime the owner of the account is free to change beneficiaries without asking the beneficiary's permission to do so.

⇨ The owner of the account is free to add to or withdraw from the account without the knowledge or consent of the beneficiary.

(Probate, Chap. XI, Sec. 438, Sec. 446, Sec. 447)

GIFT FOR THE MINOR

The ITF and POD account each solve the problem of potential liability and overreaching, but if the beneficiary of such account is a minor, there still is the problem of allowing a child access to a significant amount of money. For property located in this state, the problem is solved by applying the TEXAS UNIFORM TRANSFERS TO MINORS ACT. The law gives the owner of a bank account the right to name a person or a financial institution to be custodian of an account in the event that the owner dies before the beneficiary of the account reaches 21. For example:

Patricia Barry POD Friendly Bank
As CUSTODIAN for Frank Barry, Jr. under the
TEXAS UNIFORM TRANSFERS TO MINORS ACT.

Once Patricia dies, the monies in the account go to the bank as custodian. If Frank is 21 or older, the bank will give him the money. If he is not yet 21, the bank will hold the money for him until his 21th birthday (Property Sec. 141.004, Sec. 141.021).

The bank can deliver or spend as much of the money for Frank's care as they think advisable. If there is a disagreement about using the funds, then Frank's parent or guardian (or Frank himself if he is 14 or older) can ask a court to order that the bank use monies for Frank's care (Property Sec. 141.015).

The same law can be used to transfer securities, life insurance policies, even real property to a minor. The custodian does have the right to charge a reasonable fee for their efforts, so you need to check with the custodian to find out how they intend to handle the funds and the estimated cost of doing so (Property 141.016).

TRANSFERRING SECURITIES

You can hold a stock, or bond, or a securities brokerage account jointly with another, but with the same problems as described previously. Happily, there is a statute for securities similar to the PAY-ON-DEATH statute for banks. You can instruct the holder of the security to transfer the security to a named beneficiary once you die. You can use the POD designation or you can use a TRANSFER ON DEATH ("TOD") designation.

The law governing TOD accounts are the same as those of the POD account:

⇨ The beneficiary does not have access to the security until the owner dies. The owner of the security is free to change beneficiaries without asking the beneficiary's permission to do so.

If you wish you can hold the security jointly with rights of survivorship. The same laws apply with a TOD designation as with the POD designation, namely:

⇨ If one joint owner dies, the other owns the security outright. The surviving owner has the right to change the beneficiary of the security.

⇨ If no beneficiary survives the owner, then the security goes to the estate of the last surviving owner of the account.

(Probate Chap. XI, Sec. 450).

If you own a business, be it a sole proprietorship, partnership or small corporation, you need to make provision for the orderly transfer of your business interest in the event you die suddenly. An attorney who is experienced in business law (corporation, banking, bankruptcy, commercial law, franchise law, etc.) can offer suggestions as to the best method of ensuring that the business continues its operation, or terminates in an orderly fashion — whichever is applicable in your case.

If you cannot afford to employ an attorney at this time, then consult with your accountant. Let your accountant know who is to have access to your business records in the event of your incapacity or death. Discuss how company debts will be paid and how best to distribute the company assets to your heirs, in case of your death. If it is your intent that the business continue in your absence, you might consider purchasing key man insurance on your life to compensate the company for any loss suffered because of your absence. See page 42 for an explanation of key man insurance.

REAL PROPERTY

As explained in Chapter 5, if you own real property together with another, then who will own the property upon your death depends on how the Grantee is identified on the face of the deed. If you compare the Grantee clause of the deed to the examples on pages 98 through 103 you can determine who will inherit that property should you die. If you are not satisfied with the way the property will be inherited, then you need to consult with an attorney to change the deed so that it will conform to your wishes.

If you own the property in your name only, then once you die, there will need to be a probate procedure to determine the proper beneficiary of that parcel of land. If your main objective is to avoid probate, then you can have an attorney change the deed so that once you die, the property descends to your beneficiary without the need for probate. As with bank and securities accounts there are different ways to do so, each with its own advantages and disadvantages.

JOINT OWNERSHIP

You can have your deed changed so that you and a beneficiary are joint owners of the property with rights of survivorship. If you do so you will avoid probate of the property but you will not be able to sell that property during your lifetime without the permission of the joint owner. And if the joint owner gives permission and the property is sold, the joint owner will have the legal right to half of the proceeds of the sale.

CAUTION   GIFT OF HOMESTEAD

Some people think it a good idea to simply transfer their home to their child to avoid probate, and continue to live there. But this just creates a new set of problems:

☒ RISK OF LOSS

If you transfer your homestead to a beneficiary it could be lost if the beneficiary runs into serious financial difficulties or gets sued. This is especially a risk if your child is a professional (doctor, accountant, financial planner, attorney, nurse etc.). If your child is found to be personally liable for damages, then the house could become part of the settlement of that law suit.

If your child is (or gets) married, then this complicates matters even more so. If the child gets divorced, the property will certainly be included as part of the settlement agreement. This may be to your child's detriment because the child may need to share the value of the property with his ex-spouse. If you do not transfer the property, then it cannot become part of the marital equation.

⊠ POSSIBLE LOSS OF GOVERNMENT BENEFITS

If you transfer property, then depending upon the value of the transfer, you could be disqualified from receiving Medicaid or Supplemental Security Income ("SSI") benefits for up to 3 years from the date of transfer. The federal and state rules that determine the period of ineligibility are complex. If nursing care may be an issue in the future, then it is best to consult with an Elder Law attorney to prepare a Medicaid Estate Plan.

⊠ LOSS OF HOMESTEAD TAX EXEMPTION

If you are eligible for a general Homestead exemption or a special exemption because you are a Disabled Veteran or Senior Citizen and you make a gift of your home, you will lose your exemption. Unless the beneficiary lives in the homestead with you, and is eligible for his/her own homestead tax exemption because of age or disability, it will probably cost more in taxes to live in your own home.

You can avoid losing your homestead tax exemption by transferring the property to a beneficiary and keeping a LIFE ESTATE for yourself. But, as with joint ownership you will not be able to sell the property during your lifetime without the permission of all of the people you named as Grantee on the deed; and if you sell the property each Grantee is entitled to some portion of the proceeds of the sale (Tax 11.13(a),(j)).

OTHER TAX CONCERNS

Before you make a real estate transfer be it joint interest, life estate or outright gift, you need to consider the tax consequences of the transfer:

☒   POSSIBLE CAPITAL GAINS TAX

If you gift your homestead to your child and continue to live there until you die, then when the child sells the property there might be a capital gains tax. The child will be taxed on the increase in value from the day you bought the property.

If you don't transfer your home and the child inherits the property, he/she inherits it at the market value as of your date of death. The child can sell the property at that time without any tax consequence.

☒   POSSIBLE GIFT TAX

If the value of the transfer is worth more than $10,000 you need to file a gift tax return. For most of us, this is not a problem because no gift tax needs to be paid unless the value of the property (plus the value of all gifts in excess of $10,000 that you gave over your lifetime) exceed the estate tax credit (see the schedule on page 36). But if you are in that tax bracket, then you need to be aware that you are "using up" your tax credit.

 **LAWYER**   OUT OF STATE PROPERTY

Each state is in charge of the way property located in that state is transferred. If you own property in another state (or country) then you need to consult with an attorney in that state (or country) to determine how that property will be transferred to your beneficiaries once you die. Most state laws are similar to Texas, namely, property held as JOINT TENANTS WITH RIGHTS OF SURVIVORSHIP or a LIFE ESTATE INTEREST goes to your beneficiary without the need for probate.

If you own property in another state in your name only, or as a TENANT IN COMMON, or if you hold property jointly with your spouse in a community property state, then a probate procedure will probably need to be held in that state. If it is necessary for your heirs to have a probate procedure in Texas, then they will need an *ancillary* (secondary) procedure in the state in which the property is located. This may have the effect of doubling the cost of probate to your heirs.

Still another problem is the matter of taxes. The Texas Inheritance tax is tied to the Federal Estate tax. If your estate is too small to pay Federal Estate taxes then you pay no Texas Inheritance tax. This may not be the case with other states, so in addition to paying extra for the second probate procedure, your heirs may need to pay inheritance taxes in the state where the property is located. In such cases, you may wish to consult with an attorney for suggestions about how to set up your estate plan to avoid these problems.

A TRUST MAY BE THE ANSWER (or not)

Many of the ways to avoid probate involve methods with undesirable trade-offs. One way to avoid some of these potential problems is to set up a trust. If you have substantial assets, then you probably have heard this suggestion from your financial planner or attorney, or accountant. Even people of fairly modest means are being encouraged by these professionals to use a trust as the basis of their estate plan. But even trusts have their downside. But before getting into that, let's first discuss what a trust is and how it works:

SETTING UP A TRUST

To create a trust, an attorney prepares the trust document in accordance with the client's needs and desires. The person who signs the document is referred to as the *Grantor* or *Settlor* of the Trust. The trust document identifies who is to be the Trustee (caretaker) of property placed in the trust. Usually the Grantor appoints himself as Trustee so that he is in total control of property that he places into the trust. The trust document names a Successor Trustee who will take over the management of the trust property should the Trustee become disabled or die.

Once the trust document is signed, the Grantor transfers property into the trust. The Grantor does this by changing the name on the account from that of the Grantor to that of the Trustee. For example, if Ann Lee sets up a trust naming herself as trustee, and she wishes to place her bank account into the trust then all she need do is instruct the bank to change the name on the account from ANN LEE to ANN LEE, TRUSTEE of the ANN LEE TRUST dated April 2, 2000. Once the change is made, all the money in the bank account becomes trust property. Ann (wearing her trustee hat) still has total control of the account, taking money out, and putting money in, as she sees fit.

The trust document states how the trust property is to be managed during Ann's lifetime. If the trust is a Revocable Living Trust, then it will say that Ann has the power to terminate the trust at any time and have all trust property returned to her. Should Ann become disabled or die, then her Successor Trustee will take possession of the trust funds and manage (or distribute them) according the to direction Ann gave in the trust document. If the trust says that once Ann dies, the property is to be given to her beneficiary, then the Successor Trustee will do so; and in most cases without a probate procedure. If the trust directs the Successor Trustee to hold property in trust to care for a member of the Ann's family, then the Successor Trustee will do so.

THE GOOD PART

Setting up a trust has many good features.

☆ AVOID GUARDIANSHIP PROCEDURES

If you become disabled or too aged to handle your finances, then you do not need to worry about who takes care of your finances. Your trust appoints a Successor Trustee to take over the care of your trust if you are unable to do so. If you do not have a trust and you become incapacitated, a court may need to appoint a guardian to take care of your property. The cost to establish and maintain the guardianship is charged to you. Guardianship procedures are expensive and once established cannot be terminated unless you die or are restored to health.

☆ PRIVACY

Your trust is a private document. No one but your trustee and your beneficiaries need ever read it. If you leave property in a Will and there is a probate procedure, the Will is filed with the court. The Will becomes a public document. All can see who you did (or did not) provide for in your Will.

☆ AVOID PROBATE

Probate can be very expensive for a large estate. Both the Personal Representative and his attorney are entitled to reasonable fees. It may be necessary to hire accountants and appraisers, as well. If you have property in two states, then two probate procedures may be necessary (one in each state) and that could be costly. If the trust is properly drafted and your property placed into the trust, you may be able to avoid probate altogether.

☆ CARE FOR A CHILD OR FAMILY MEMBER:

If you make provision in your trust to care for a child or a family member after you die, then your Successor Trustee can do so. If the family member is someone who is immature or a born spender, you can set up a Spendthrift Trust to protect the family member from squandering his inheritance. The Successor Trustee can see to it that the trust funds are used to pay for the family member's education or living expenses, and nothing more.

☆ TAX SAVINGS:

There can be substantial Estate tax savings if you are married and you and your spouse each set up your own trust. For example, suppose you and your spouse together have an estate worth one million dollars. You can each set up your own trust with $500,000. Each trust can provide that if one of you dies, the surviving spouse can use the income from the deceased partner's trust for living expenses. Once the second partner dies, all of the monies in the two trusts can be distributed, with no estate taxes due on either trust. By doing this, you each take advantage of your own Estate and Gift Tax Exclusion. If you don't separate the funds and one of you dies, the surviving spouse has all of the money with only one deduction. For example, if the Exclusion amount is $675,000 and Estate tax rate is 37%, then the beneficiaries will pay over $120,000 in Estate taxes.

THE PROBLEMS

For married people of means, it makes good sense to establish a trust. Others need to consider the downside:

⊠ COMPLEXITY

A trust is a fairly complex document, often 20 pages long. It needs to be that long because you are establishing a vehicle for taking care of your property during your lifetime, as well as after your death. The trust usually is written in "legalese," so it may take you considerable time and effort to understand it. It is important to work with an attorney who has the patience to work with you until you fully understand each paragraph of the document and are satisfied that this is what you want.

⊠ COST

Because of the complexity of the document and the fact that it is custom designed for you, a trust will cost much more to draft than a simple Will. In addition to the initial cost of the trust, it can be expensive to maintain the trust should you become disabled or die. Your Successor Trustee has the right to charge for his duties as trustee, as well as to charge for any specialized services performed. For example, if you choose an attorney to be Successor Trustee, then the attorney has the right to charge to manage the trust, and also charge for any legal work he performs. A financial institution can charge to serve as Successor Trustee, and also charge to manage the trust portfolio (Property Sec. 114.061).

These charges can be considerable. Before appointing someone as Successor Trustee, you need to investigate what the Successor Trustee will charge to manage the trust.

⊠ NO CREDITOR PROTECTION

Because property held in a Revocable Living Trust is freely accessible to the Grantor, it is likewise accessible to his creditors both before and after the Grantor's death. If the Grantor dies owing money then the trust funds can be used to pay for those debts.

⊠ TAXES MAY STILL BE A PROBLEM:

While the Grantor is operating the trust as Trustee, all of the property held in a Revocable Living Trust is taxed as if the Grantor were holding that property in his/her own name. If the value of the trust property exceeds the Estate and Gift Tax Exclusion amount (see page 36 for the value), then unless the Grantor takes some other, more advanced, Estate Planning strategies taxes will be due and owing once the Grantor dies.

⊠ PROBATE MIGHT STILL BE NECESSARY

The trust only works for those items that you place in the trust. If you have property that is held jointly with another, then when you die, that property will go to the joint owner and not to the trust. If you purchase a security in your name only, and forget to put it in your trust, there will need to be a probate procedure to determine the beneficiary of that security.

MAYBE PROBATE ISN'T ALL THAT BAD

As explained, if you hold all of your property in trust or jointly with another, you may be able to avoid probate and have your property go directly to your heirs. But you may have reason not to choose either of these methods. Perhaps you don't have money at this time to pay an attorney to set up a trust.

Maybe you do not want to hold your money jointly with anyone because you are concerned about losing your independence or maybe you are concerned about keeping your money secure. Still another concern may be that if the joint owner is married then the spouse of the joint owner may have a right to some portion of that joint account according to the laws of the state where they live.

Still another reason for not holding property jointly is to be sure that your property is distributed in the way that you wish and according to the directions in your Will. If you want your money to go to several charities or to a minor child, then you may decide that it is better to make a Will rather than hold money jointly with just verbal instructions to your beneficiary about how you want the funds distributed when you die.

For example, if you hold all of your property jointly with your child, then the child is the legal owner of your property as of your date of death. If you tell your child to use some of that money for your grandchild's education, then that puts an unreasonable burden on your child because you were not specific as to exactly how much of that joint account was to be used for the child's education. Also you did not say how to use the money. Is the money for tuition only? Can the money be used to pay the child's living expenses?

Even if you give your child specific instructions about how the money is to be spent, and even if your child is honorable and with the best intentions, it may be that your grandchild gets none of the money, because your child is sued or falls upon hard times and is forced to use that money to pay debts. If you keep your property in your own name and leave a Will giving a certain amount of money for your grandchild, then he/she will know exactly how much money you left and the purpose of that gift.

If your grandchild is a minor at the time you make your Will you can appoint someone in your Will to be a custodian of the child's gift under The Texas Uniform Transfers to Minor's Act. As discussed at the beginning of this chapter, the custodian can be a person (such as the child's parent) or trust company or financial institution. You can direct the custodian to keep the property in trust until the child reaches 18, or if you wish until the child reaches 21.

If you have a Will, and hold all of your money in your name only, then it will be distributed according to the directions you give in your Will. If you specify that the probate of your Will is to be supervised by the court, then any deviation from the instructions in your Will can be made only for good cause and with court approval.

PREPARING A WILL

Some people think they do not need to prepare a Will until they are very old and about to die. But according to reports published by the National Center for Health Statistics (a division of the U.S. Department of Health and Human Services) 2 of every 10 people who die in any given year are under the age of 60. Many will think that 20% is a small number until it hits close to home as it did with a young couple who were having difficulty conceiving a child. They went from doctor to doctor until they met someone just beginning his practice. With his knowledge of the latest advances in medicine, he was able to help them. The birth of their child was a moment of joy and gratitude. They asked a nurse to take a picture of them all together — the happy couple, the newborn child and the doctor who made it all happen. Happiness radiated from the picture, but one of them would be dead within six months.

You might think it was the child. An infant's life is so fragile. SIDS and all manner of childhood diseases can threaten a little one.
No, he grew up to be a healthy young man.

If you looked at the picture, you might guess the husband. Overweight and stressed out; his ruddy complexion suggested high blood pressure. He looked like a typical heart- attack-prone type A personality.
No, he was fine and went on to enjoy raising his son.

Probably the wife. She had such a difficult time with the pregnancy and the delivery was especially hard. Perhaps it was all too much for her.
No, she recovered and later had two more children.

It was the doctor who was killed in a three car collision.

Though we all agree, that one never knows, still many procrastinate, rationalizing that if they die, Texas law will take over and their property will be distributed in the manner that they would have wanted anyway. The problem with that reasoning is the complexity of the Rules of Descent and Distribution. If you are survived by a spouse, child, parent or sibling, then it isn't too difficult to figure out who will inherit your property. But if none of these survive you, the ultimate beneficiary of your property may not be the person you would have chosen, had you taken the time to do so. Also consider that the probate procedure is more expensive and time consuming when there is no Will.

Others think that no Will is necessary because they have arranged their finances so that all of their property goes to their intended beneficiary automatically and without the need for probate. But it could happen that you die as a result of an accident, and someone will need to be appointed as your Personal Representative to sue on behalf of your estate. It is better to leave a Will so that you can say who will be in charge of handling your affairs once you die (your Personal Representative). If you don't have a Will and a probate procedure is necessary then the Probate court will choose someone for the job (see Page 27 for those with priority to serve).

Still another benefit to making a Will is that you can make provision for who will get your personal property, including your car. Without a Will, your Personal Representative gets to make these decisions. With a Will you can make special provision for the care of your child or grandchild. You can even provide for the care of your pet as these next few pages will show.

MAKE A GIFT OF YOUR CAR

As explained in Chapter 6, if you are married in hold title to the car with your spouse with right of survivorship, then all your spouse need do is to take the title to the car and a certified copy of the death certificate to the local County Tax Assessor-Collectors office and change the title to that of the spouse.

If you are not holding the car jointly with rights of survivorship, then consider making a gift of your car in your Will. If you do so, then it will be relatively simple for your car to be transferred to the beneficiary. If you do not make a specific gift of your car in your Will, then it becomes part of your probate estate. Your Personal Representative can sell the car and include the proceeds of the sale in the estate funds to be distributed to your residuary beneficiaries. If all of the residuary beneficiaries agree, the Representative can give the car to one of them as part of that beneficiary's share of the estate. If you die intestate, the car will go to your next of kin.

JOINT OWNERSHIP
Some may think it just as easy to hold the car jointly with the intended beneficiary, so that when one owner dies, the other owns the car without any need for probate — but the problem with joint ownership of a motor vehicle is liability. If either owner is in an accident with the car, then both may be liable for any damage that is done. If you are single, the better route is to hold title to the car in your name only and make a gift of the car in your Will.

FOR PET LOVERS

A woman died at peace,
leaving her fortune
and care of her cat to her niece.
Alas, the fortune and the cat
Soon disappeared after that.

You could make provision in your Will for the care of your pet, but the moral of the above limerick, is that leaving your money to someone to do the job may not be the best route to go.

   TRUST FOR CARE OF PET

If you are serious about caring for your pet after your death, you can employ an attorney to set up a separate trust for the care of your pet, or you can have the attorney include a trust provision in your Will. The trust document will direct the trustee to pay sufficient monies to a custodian for the care of the pet. You also need to name a beneficiary (a person or charitable organization) to receive whatever monies remaining in the trust once the pet dies.

The Texas Society for Prevention of Cruelty to Animals ("SPCA") has a Planned Giving Program that offers life care for the pet in exchange for a bequest to the SPCA. For information about the program you can call your local SPCA.

CARE OF PETS (Continued)

If you don't have the resources to set up a trust to care for your pet, you can still ask a fellow pet lover to care for the animal. If no one among your circle of family and friends is able to do so, then ask your pet's veterinarian to consider starting an "Orphaned Pet Service" to assist in finding new homes for pets who lose their owners. It is good public relations and a potential source of income. People can make provision in their Will to pay the Veterinarian to care for the pet until a suitable family can be found. That is a more humane approach than the, all too common practice, of putting a pet "to sleep" rather than have the pet suffer the loss of its master. And in at least one case, that reasoning backfired.

Eleanor always had a pet in the house. After her husband died, her two poodles were her constant companions. When Eleanor became ill with cancer, she worried about what would happen to her "buddies" if she died. She finally decided it best to have her family put them to sleep when she died.

Eleanor endured surgery, chemotherapy, radiation therapy, and even some holistic remedies, but she continued to go downhill. Eleanor's family came in to visit her at the hospital to say their last good-byes. She was so ill, she didn't even recognize them. No one thought she could last the day. Because the family was from out of state, and time short, they decided to put the pets to sleep so they need only take care of the funeral arrangements when she died. To everyone's surprise, Eleanor rallied. She lived two more long, lonely years. She often said she wished they had put her to sleep instead of her buddies.

PROVIDING FOR THE CHILD

Parents have a special responsibility. They need to make provision for the care of their child in the event they both die or become incapacitated before the child is grown. If one parent dies, then the other has the right (and duty) to care for the child. If they both die, then it is important that the parent make provision for who will care for their minor child. Under Texas law, it is relatively simple to make that provision.

APPOINTING A GUARDIAN

A child must be cared for in two ways, the *person* of the child and *property* of the child. To care for the person of the child, someone must be in charge of the child's everyday living, not only food and shelter but to provide social, ethical and religious training. Someone must have legal authority to make medical decisions and see to the child's education. To care for the property of the child, someone must take charge of monies left to the child. That person is responsible to see that the monies are used for the care of the child and that anything left over is preserved until the child becomes an adult.

Texas statute gives a parent the right to name a guardian to care for the person and property of his/her minor child. The parent can make this appointment by signing a form entitled: DECLARATION OF APPOINTMENT OF GUARDIAN
FOR MY CHILDREN IN THE EVENT OF MY DEATH
The statutory form of the Declaration (Probate Chap. XIII, Sec. 677A (e)) can be found in any law library or you can download it from the Internet (see page 166 for the Texas statute Web site). It is important that you confer with the other parent of the child, because if you choose different people and then die simultaneously, the judge gets to choose who to appoint as guardian (Probate, Chap. XIII, Sec. 676).

You can include the Declaration as an addition to your Will, or you can sign it as a separate document. The Declaration should be kept with your Will or other important papers while you are alive. Should a guardian need to be appointed, then the Declaration needs to be filed with the court when the court is in the process of appointing a legal guardian for the child. In appointing a guardian, the judge's primary concern is the best interests of the child. The judge will give priority to the person you chose as Guardian, but if the judge determines that person is not qualified to be the child's guardian, he will appoint someone who is. Once the child is 12 years of age, the child can ask the court to appoint the guardian of the child's choice. If the person chosen by the child is qualified to serve as guardian, and the circumstances warrant, the court can appoint that person to serve as your child's guardian (Probate Chap. XIII, Sec. 676, 677, 680).

LEAVING PROPERTY FOR THE CHILD

As any parent is well aware, it is expensive to raise a child. People that you might consider to be the best choice to serve as your child's guardian might not be able to do so unless you leave sufficient monies to pay for the care of the child. If you are a person of limited finances, then consider purchasing a term life insurance policy on your life and/or on the life of the other parent of the child. If you can only afford one policy, then insure the life of the parent who contributes most to the support of the child.

Term insurance policies are relatively inexpensive if you limit the term to just that period of time until your child becomes an adult. Some companies offer a combination of term life and disability insurance. As with any other purchase, it is important to comparison shop to obtain the best price for the coverage.

FOR PARENTS OF A MINOR CHILD (continued)

If you are married to the parent of your child, then the beneficiary of the term insurance policy can be your spouse with your child as an alternate beneficiary. Married or single, you can name your child as the primary beneficiary of the policy. If you name the child as beneficiary of the policy that is $50,000 or less in value, and you die before the child turns 18, the insurance company can turn over the insurance proceeds to the Clerk of the probate court. The Clerk will hold the monies and keep them invested according to Texas law, until the child is 18.

Anytime before the child's 18th birthday, whoever is the custodian of the child can ask the court to allow the monies to be used for the support of the child. Once the child turns 18, the court will supervise the distribution of the monies to the child (Probate Chap. XIII, Sec. 745 and 887).

If the amount of funds inherited by a minor child exceed $50,000, then the court will appoint a guardian of the child's property. Guardianship proceedings can be time-consuming and expensive. If you are planning to leave a significant amount of insurance funds to your child then the better route might be to name a custodian for the insurance funds under the UNIFORM TRANSFERS TO MINORS ACT (see page 176) or you can consult with an attorney about setting up a trust for the child as is explained on the next page.

 **LAWYER** | PREPARE A TRUST FOR THE CHILD

If you have sufficient monies to care for your child until adulthood, then consult with an attorney about setting up a trust for the child or drafting a Will with a trust provision in the event you die before the child is grown. You will need to appoint a trustee to handle the trust funds as the child is growing. You can appoint the other parent of the child as the trustee. You will need to appoint a successor trustee in the event that the other parent is unable to serve as trustee.

You can appoint the same person to serve as trustee as you have chosen to serve as Standby Guardian, but it may be better to appoint two different people for these jobs. The desirable qualities of a guardian are essentially that of a "people person" someone who is sensitive to the child's emotional needs — someone who will love and nurture the child.

The qualities of importance in a trustee are honesty, trustworthiness and being knowledgeable in money matters. The trustee will be in charge of giving sufficient money to the guardian for the child's maintenance. Consider choosing a trustee who is not overly generous so that all of the funds will be spent before the child is grown, yet not so thrifty that the child has little quality of life in his formative years.

If you are successful in your choice, the child will be fortunate to have two such adults to guide him through his childhood.

PROVIDING FOR THE STEPCHILD

Perhaps the reason that the story of Cinderella has such universal appeal, is that many stepchildren, at one point or another, feel left out. Even the law seems to reinforce that perception. For example, if you have a stepchild and you die without a Will, then that child has no intestate rights to your estate. If you and your spouse hold all property jointly with rights of survivorship, and your spouse dies first, then your stepchild will be left nothing unless you make some provision for the child in your Will.

Should your spouse die, then you, and not your stepchild, have the authority to agree to an autopsy or an anatomical gift. Even during your spouse's lifetime, you, and not your stepchild, have the authority to make your spouse's medical decisions in the event that your spouse becomes incapacitated.

Of course, giving you authority to make your spouse's medical decisions and giving you the right to inherit all of your spouse's estate must be a decision that is agreeable to your spouse. If your spouse wants his/her child to have primary authority to make medical decisions, then your spouse can sign a Medical Power of Attorney and appoint the child (and not you) as Health Care Agent. Similarly, if your spouse wants his/her child to inherit property, then your spouse can arrange his/her finances so that the child will inherit property. Hopefully, your spouse will consult with an estate planning attorney who can explain the best way to achieve that goal, else that intent could be thwarted and the child end up with much less than intended, as was the case in the example given on page 118.

PROVIDING FOR THE ADULT CHILD

It isn't just stepchildren who can be left out if no provision is made. Even children from a long-standing marriage can be cut off against the wishes of a parent. A parent may assume that all of their children will be treated equally once they are both gone, but consider that the last to die is the one who gets to decide "who gets what." That was the case with Joan and Herbert. They were a devoted couple, married over forty years. Herb was the breadwinner, but he was content to let Joan handle all of the finances.

Joan wanted to be sure that each of their three daughters would always have a decent place to live. They purchased a three story house and each of the daughters moved into a different floor of the home. It was the parent's intent that once they were both gone, the daughters would inherit and occupy the property.

The couple held everything jointly with rights of survivorship. When Joan died, all of their property, including the home, was owned by Herbert. The grief suffered by Herbert at his wife's passing was more than he could bear. He alternated between sadness, despair and anger.

His middle daughter took the brunt of his anger. Their relationship had always been strained. She felt she could never live up to her father's expectations. She was not the cute baby of the family as was her younger sister. She was not the eldest daughter who always seemed to make her Dad proud. He always made her feel that she was a disappointment to him. Once her mother died, she had no one left to buffer the relationship with her father.

Within three months of Joan's death, Herbert had an attorney draft a Will leaving all to his eldest and youngest daughter. None of the children knew what he had done.

Herbert decided to take a trip to Europe to try to escape the pain of his mourning. When he was in France, he suffered a massive heart attack and died. It was less than 6 months from the date of Joan's death.

Had he returned from Europe, he may have reconciled with his daughter, but as it happened, there was no time for them to develop a better relationship.

With both their parents gone, the eldest and youngest daughter decided to sell the home. The youngest sister offered two thousand dollars of the proceeds to the middle daughter. The middle daughter refused the offer with unkind words. Being offered less than her one-third share, meant to her, that her sisters approved of their father's action. It was as if she were being disinherited all over again.

It was unfortunate that Joan's best plans were thwarted. They didn't have to be. She and Herbert could have kept a life estate in the property with the remainder going to all three girls. That would have ensured that each daughter received an equal inheritance. More importantly, the family would not have been torn by the hurt and anger that was more a product of a husband's grief rather than the absence of a father's love.

 **A SPECIAL NEEDS TRUST FOR THE INCAPACITATED**

If a person is incapacitated, both the federal and state government provide assistance with programs such as social security disability benefits and custodial nursing home care under the Medicaid program. The family often supplements the government program by providing for the incapacitated person's *special needs*, such as clothing, hobbies, special education, outings to a movie or special event — things that give the incapacitated person some quality of life.

To be eligible for government assistance programs the incapacitated must be essentially without funds. Caretakers fear that leaving money to the incapacitated in a will or trust will disqualify the incapacitated from further government assistance. Understanding this dilemma, the federal government allows caretakers to set up a *Special Needs* trust with the incapacitated as the beneficiary of the trust. One type of Special Needs Trust is the *Disability Trust* as authorized by 42 U.S.C. 1382c(a)(3). This trust may be established by a caretaker for an incapacitated person who is under the age of 65. A trustee is appointed to use trust funds to provide for the special needs of the incapacitated. If any trust funds are left after the incapacitated dies, then those funds must be used to reimburse the state for monies spent on behalf of the incapacitated person.

There are other types of special needs trusts that are allowed under the law. An experienced Elder Law attorney can explain the different options available and assist the family member in preparing a Will or trust that will provide for the incapacitated person's special needs once the family member dies.

 **LAWYER**

PROVIDING FOR THE INCAPACITATED

If you are the caretaker or legal guardian of someone who is incapacitated, then in addition to preparing your own estate plan, you need to be concerned about what will happen to the incapacitated person should you die. Someone will need to make medical decisions for the incapacitated person and see to it that he/she is properly housed and fed.

APPOINTMENT OF A SUCCESSOR CARETAKER

Often a family member will agree to take responsibility for the care of an incapacitated person in the event that the caretaker dies. But perhaps no one wants the job, or the opposite case, too many want to have control. For example, if a parent is incapacitated, one child may want the parent to remain at home with the assistance of a home health care worker. Another child may think the best place for the parent is an assisted living facility with 24 hour care. The caretaker spouse may be concerned that a tug-of-war will erupt once he dies.

In such case, the caretaker should consult with an attorney to ensure future care for the incapacitated person. The attorney may suggest establishing a trust or having a legal guardian appointed for the incapacitated person while the parent/caretaker is alive. Once the guardianship is in place, the court will continue to supervise the care of the incapacitated person until he/she dies.

PROVIDING FOR YOUR OWN INCAPACITY

As the life expectancy of the population increases, so does the percentage of the population who suffer from debilitating diseases such Alzheimer's and Parkinsons'. As you age, your chances for suffering dementia as a result of a stroke or other debilitating diseases increases. It is estimated that more than 50% of the population who are 85 or older, suffer some degree of dementia. If you are concerned that you may become disabled in the future, you need to consider who will care for your property and who will take care of your person.

CARING FOR YOUR PROPERTY

If you have significant assets, you can have an attorney prepare a trust. You can be trustee of the funds while you have capacity. Once you can no longer do so, then the person you name as Successor Trustee will take over.

If you do not have sufficient assets to justify the cost of a trust, then consider appointing someone to be your Agent to handle your finances in the event of your incapacity. You can do this by signing a document called a Durable Power of Attorney. Your attorney can prepare the Durable Power of Attorney to meet your special needs or you can use the statutory form provided by the state of Texas (Probate Chap. XII, Sec. 490). You can find this statute at any law library or you can download it from the Texas Statute Web site (see page 166).

CARING FOR YOUR PERSON

You can appoint someone to be your guardian in the event of your later incapacity by signing a document called:

**DECLARATION OF GUARDIAN IN THE EVENT
OF LATER INCAPACITY OR NEED OF GUARDIAN.**

You can get the statutory form of the Declaration (Probate Chap. XIII, Sec. 678) at any law library or you can download it from the Texas statute Web site (see page 166). If you ever need a guardian of your person or property, then the person you chose to serve as guardian can file the Declaration with the Probate court. The judge will appoint the person you chose as guardian unless the court finds that he/she is not qualified to serve. For example, the court will not appoint someone who has been convicted of aggravated assault, or of having injured an elderly person.

The person appointed as the guardian of your person has the job of supervising your everyday care and seeing to it that you receive proper nursing care. There may be no reason to have someone appointed as your legal guardian if your family is caring for you and you have given someone written authority to make your medical decisions in the event that you are too ill to do so yourself. As explained in Chapter 7, you can appoint a Health Care Agent by signing a Medical Power of Attorney for Health Care. It is also important to sign a Directive to let your Agent know whether you do (or do not) want life support systems to be applied in the event that you are too ill to make your own medical decisions and are about to die.

If you appoint someone to handle your finances and make your medical decisions, then there should be no need for your family to go through the costly and time-consuming effort of have a legal guardian appointed in the event of your incapacity.

When people draft a Will they are more concerned about giving their possessions away than they are about taking into account what they actually have to give. This was the case with Larry. He had no family except a distant cousin, and he lost track of him years ago. After his wife died, he bought a condominium in Laredo. Over the years, he developed a close network of friends. They became his family. Larry did not have much money. His car was leased. He had a mortgage on the condominium. He wanted his friends to know how much they meant to him so he had a Will drafted just before he died giving all he owned to five close friends.

The friends appreciated the gesture but the probate procedure turned out to be a nightmare. They had to keep current the mortgage payments and the maintenance fees until the condominium was sold. Because Larry left little cash, this money had to come out of the beneficiaries' pockets. Two were living on their social security income and they had to borrow money from the others to contribute to their share of the upkeep.

The beneficiaries had no money to settle the lease on the car. Even if they did, they decided that there was no point in doing so because the amount needed to obtain clear title was greater than the current market value of the car. The beneficiaries decided not to make any further payment and they returned the car to the leasing agent. Their decision turned out to be a losing proposition. The leasing agent took the car, sold it and then sued the estate for the balance of the monies owed on the lease.

Because the beneficiaries had to quickly liquidate the estate, the condominium sold for less than it would have had they the time, energy and resources to fix it up. After they settled with the leasing agent, paid off the funeral expenses, mortgage, and probate fees there was only a few hundred dollars left. That was a lot of work and stress for nothing.

The pity was that Larry could have arranged his finances so that his beneficiaries were not burdened by his debt. He could have taken out mortgage insurance as part of the loan package. In most cases the cost of the insurance is nominal and is included as part of the monthly mortgage payment.

Larry could have done the same when he leased the car. Most leasing contracts offer term life insurance as an option. The cost of such insurance depends on the age of the person, the term of the loan and the amount of monies owed, but the premium paid each month is just a small fraction of the loan payment.

Even if Larry just arranged for payment of one of these debts, his beneficiaries would have come away with the gift that Larry intended, instead of the headache that they inherited.

PROVIDE FOR CREDIT CARD DEBT

If you have significant credit card debt, you need to consider how that debt will be paid once you die. Most credit card companies offer insurance policies and include the premium as part of your monthly payment. If you have such insurance, then should you die, any outstanding balance is paid. It benefits the credit card company to offer life insurance as part of the credit package, because they are assured of prompt payment should the borrower die. However, if you have little or no assets and no one other than yourself is liable to pay the debt, you may have no incentive to pay for insurance that can only benefit the lender.

As discussed in Chapters 2 and 4, if you hold a credit card jointly with another person, both of you are equally liable to pay the debt. If one of you dies, the other is responsible to pay the bill regardless of who ran up the bill. If paying that bill could be a struggle for the surviving debtor, then the better route to go is for each of you to have your own credit card.

Still another reason not to hold a joint credit card is that each of you can establish your own line of credit. This is especially important if you are married and one of you is retired or has been out of the job market for any period of time. Should the breadwinner die, it may be difficult for the surviving partner to establish credit if he/she has no recent work record It is easier for the unemployed spouse to establish a line of credit when he/she is married to someone who is working.

PURCHASING LIFE INSURANCE

The good part of purchasing loan insurance — be it credit card insurance, mortgage insurance or car insurance, is that you can usually purchase the insurance without taking a medical examination. The down side is that such insurance may be more expensive than a life insurance policy. If you are in fairly good health, consider taking out a life insurance policy to cover all of your outstanding loans. The cost of the single life insurance policy may be significantly less than purchasing separate loan insurance policies.

The estate planning strategy of purchasing life insurance to pay off all of your loans works best if you are married and your spouse is jointly liable for your debts. If you name your spouse as beneficiary of the life insurance policy, then he/she can use the life insurance funds to pay off all monies owed. If you name someone as beneficiary who has no legal obligation to pay your debts and if your primary residence is in the state of Texas, none of your creditors can force your beneficiary to use any part of those funds to pay your debts (Insurance 21.22).

If you want the insurance funds used to pay your debts, then this may not be the way to go. But, if you want to be sure that someone receives money for their care after you are gone, and you do not want those funds reduced by the cost of probate or to pay off your debts, then this strategy should accomplish your goal.

Some people have an "every man for himself" attitude and are content to have no life insurance at all. Others worry about how their loved ones will manage if they are not around to support them. The same person may have different thoughts about insurance coverage as the circumstances of their life changes — from no coverage in their bachelor days to more-than-enough coverage in their child rearing days to just-enough-to-bury-me in their senior years. Insurance companies recognize that people's needs change over the years. Many companies offer flexible insurance coverage. As with any consumer item, it is a good idea to shop around.

In addition to life insurance, you might want to consider long-term health care insurance. Your best estate plan could be sabotaged by a lengthy, or debilitating illness. If you are poor, long-term nursing care may not be of concern to you, because all your needs should be covered under Medicaid. If you are very wealthy, you may not worry because you have more than enough money to pay for your care. But the rest of us need to think about ways to provide for long-term health care. An experienced Elder law attorney can suggest an estate plan that will preserve your assets in the event of a lengthy illness.

If long-term care insurance is part of your estate plan, then you need to consider the many plans that are available. You can get the publication A SHOPPER'S GUIDE TO LONG-TERM CARE INSURANCE from the National Association of Insurance Commissioners by calling (816) 842-3600. If you have specific questions about long-term care insurance, then call the Texas Department on Aging at (800) 252-9240. They also have information available at their Web site:

 TEXAS DEPARTMENT ON AGING
http://www. tdoa.state.tx.us

ANNUITIES TO SPREAD THE INHERITANCE

Most beneficiaries go through their inheritance within two years. For many, the reason the money is gone so soon, is that there just wasn't much money to inherit in the first place. But for others, it's a spending frenzy.

People's spending habits remain much the same throughout their lifetime. Some people are squirrels, always saving for the winter. For others, it's:

Earn-A-Penny   Spend-A-Penny

Most of us fall somewhere in between. We are not extravagant in our spending habits, yet it is a struggle to save. But why should we struggle to purchase an insurance policy if the intended beneficiary will spend it in a few months?

If you want to leave an insurance policy benefit to someone you love, but the intended beneficiary is immature, or a born spendthrift, then a simple solution to the problem may be to purchase an annuity. The annuity can be set up so that the beneficiary receives money on a monthly, or yearly basis, rather than a single lump sum payment when you die.

You can also purchase life insurance policies that can be paid out in installments or over a period of years, rather than in a single lump sum. There are many different types of policies available, so again, it is important to shop around.

CHOOSING THE RIGHT ESTATE PLAN

Joint Ownership?
A POD Account?
A TOD Account?
A Trust?
A Will?
An Insurance Policy???

This chapter offers so many options that the reader may be more confused than when he was blissfully unenlightened.

As with most things in life, you may find there are no ultimate solutions, just alternatives. The right choice for you is the one that best accomplishes your goal. This being the case, you first need to determine what you want to accomplish with the money that you leave. Think about what will happen to your property if you were to die suddenly, without making any plan different from the one you now have.
Who will get your property?
Will there be any estate tax?
Will they need to go through a full probate procedure?

If the answers to these questions are not what you wish, then you need to work to retitle your property to accomplish your goals. For those with significant assets, — especially those with estates large enough to pay estate taxes, a trip to an experienced Estate Planning attorney may be well worth the consultation fee.

Once you are satisfied with your estate plan, then the final thing to determine is whether your heirs will be able to locate your assets once you are deceased.

Most people have their business records in one place, their Will in another place, car titles and deeds in still another place. When someone dies, their beneficiaries may feel as if they are playing a game of "hide and seek" with the decedent. The game might be fun if it were not for the fact that things not found may be forever lost. For example, suppose you die in an accident and no one knows you are insured by your credit card company for accidental death in the amount of $25,000. The only one to profit is the insurance company, which is just that much richer because no one told them that you died as a result of an accident.

How about a key to a safe deposit box located in another state? Will anyone find it? Even if they find the key, how will they find the box?

It is not difficult to arrange things so that your affairs are always in order. It amounts to being aware of what you own (and owe) and keeping a record of your possessions. A side benefit is that by doing so, you will always know where all your business records are. If you ever spent time trying to collect information to file your taxes or trying to find a lost stock or bond certificate, you will appreciate the value of organizing your records.

GUIDING THOSE LEFT BEHIND

Heirs need all the help they can get. It is difficult enough dealing with the loss, none the less trying to locate important documents. Your heirs will have no problem locating your assets if you keep all of your records a single place. It can be a desk drawer or a file cabinet or even a shoe box. It is helpful if you keep a separate file or folder for each type of investment. You might consider setting up the following folders:

📁 THE BANK & SECURITIES FOLDER

Store your original certificates for stocks, bonds, mutual funds, certificates of deposit, in a folder labeled BANK & SECURITIES FOLDER. In addition to the original certificate include a copy of the contract you signed with each financial institution. The contract will show where you have funds and who you named as beneficiary or joint owner of the account. If someone owes you money and has signed a Promissory note or mortgage that identifies you as the lender, then you can store these documents in this folder as well.

If you wish to store your original documents in a safe deposit box, then keep a record of the location of the safe deposit box, and the number of the box, in this folder. Make a copy of all of the items stored in the box and place the copies in this folder. If you have an extra key to the box, then put the key in the folder. If you are the only person with access to the box, it may take an order from the Probate court to remove items from the box once you die. Consider allowing someone you trust to be able to gain entry to the box in the event of your incapacity or death.

📁 THE DEED FOLDER

Many people save every scrap of paper associated with the closing of real property. If you closed recently on real estate and there was a mortgage involved in the purchase, you probably walked away from closing with enough paper to wallpaper your kitchen. If you wish, you can keep all of those papers in a separate file that identifies the property, for example:

CLOSING PAPERS FOR THE GALVESTON PROPERTY.

Set aside the original deed (or a copy if the original is in a safe deposit box) and place it into a separate DEED FOLDER. Include deeds to parcels of real property, cemetery deeds, condominium deeds, cooperative shares to real property, timesharing certificates, etc. Include deeds to out of state property as well as Texas property in the DEED FOLDER. If you have a mortgage on your property, then put a copy of the mortgage and promissory note in a separate LIABILITY FOLDER.

📁 THE INSURANCE/PENSION FOLDER

The INSURANCE FOLDER is for each original insurance policy that you own, be it car insurance, homeowner's insurance or a health care insurance policy. If you purchased real property, you probably received a title commitment at closing and the original title insurance policy some weeks later when you received your original deed from recording. If you cannot locate the title insurance policy, then contact the closing agent and have them send you a copy of your title policy. If you have a pension or an annuity, then include those documents in this folder as well.

THE PERSONAL PROPERTY FOLDER

MOTOR VEHICLES
Put all motor vehicle titles in Personal Property folder. This includes cars, mobile homes, boats, planes, etc. If you owe money on the vehicle, the lender may have possession of the title certificate. If such is the case, then put a copy of the registration in this folder and a copy of the promissory note or chattel mortgage in a separate liability folder.

If you have a boat or plane, then identify the location of the motor vehicle. For example, if you are leasing space in an airplane hanger or in a marina, then keep a copy of the leasing agreement in this file.

JEWELRY
If you own expensive jewelry, then keep a picture of the item together with the sales receipt or written appraisal in this folder.

COLLECTOR'S ITEMS
If you own a valuable art collection, or a coin collection or any other item of significant value, then include a picture of the item in this file. Also include evidence of ownership of the item, such as a sales receipt or a certificate of authenticity, or a written appraisal of the property.

📁 THE LIABILITY FOLDER

The LIABILITY FOLDER should contain all loan documents of debts that you owe. For example, if you purchased real property and have a mortgage on that property, then put a copy of the mortgage and promissory note in this folder. If you owe money on a car, then put the promissory note and chattel mortgage on the car in the file. If you have a credit card, then put a copy of the contract you signed with the credit card company in this file.

Many people never take the time to calculate their **net worth** (what a person owns less what that person owes). By having a record of your outstanding debts, you can calculate your net worth whenever you wish.

📁 THE TAX RECORD FOLDER

Your Personal Representative (or next of kin) will need to file your final income tax return. Keep a copy of your tax returns (both federal and state) for the past three years in your Tax Record Folder.

THE PERSONAL RECORD FOLDER

The PERSONAL RECORD FOLDER should include documents that relate to you personally, such as a birth certificate, naturalization papers, pre-nuptial or post- nuptial agreement, Will or Trust, marriage certificate, divorce papers, army records, social security card; etc. If you have a Health Care Directive or a Power of Attorney, then this is a good place to keep those documents.

FOR FEDERAL RETIREES

If you are a Federal Retiree, then you should have received your **PERSONAL IDENTIFICATION NUMBER (PIN)** and the person who will inherit your pension (your *survivor annuitant*) should have received his/her own PIN as well. It is relatively simple to obtain this during your lifetime, but it may be difficult and/or stressful for your survivor annuitant to work through the system once you are gone. To get information on obtaining these numbers you can call the **RETIREMENT INFORMATION OFFICE** at (888) 767-6738. For the hearing impaired, call (800) 878-5707.

Upon your death, your survivor annuitant may be entitled to death benefits. These benefits are not automatic. Your survivor annuitant must apply for them by submitting a death claim to the Office of Personnel Management. Your survivor needs to know that it is necessary to apply and also how to apply. See page 30 for an explanation about how to apply for benefits and then make that information available to your family. You can either put this information in the insurance/pension folder or in your Personal Record folder.

THE *If I Die* FILE

In addition to keeping your up-to-date records in a single place, you need to let your family know the location of these items. You can set up an *If I Die* file and give that file to your next of kin or the person you appointed as Personal Representative in your Will.

You can use the form on the next page as a basis for the information to include in the file.

If I Die

then the following information will help settle my estate:

INFORMATION FOR DEATH CERTIFICATE

MY FULL LEGAL NAME _____

MY SOCIAL SECURITY NO. _____

MY USUAL OCCUPATION _____

BIRTH DATE AND BIRTH PLACE _____

If naturalized, date & place _____

MY FATHER'S NAME _____

MY MOTHER'S MAIDEN NAME _____

PERSONS TO BE NOTIFIED OF MY DEATH

_____

_____

_____

FUNERAL AND BURIAL ARRANGEMENTS

LOCATION OF BURIAL SITE

_____

LOCATION OF PRENEED FUNERAL CONTRACT

_____

FOR VETERAN or SPOUSE BURIAL IN A NATIONAL CEMETERY

BRANCH_____SERIAL NO._____

VETERAN'S RANK _____

VETERAN'S VA CLAIM NUMBER _____

DATE AND PLACE OF ENTRY INTO SERVICE:

_____

DATE AND PLACE OF SEPARATION FROM SERVICE:

_____

LOCATION OF OFFICIAL MILITARY DISCHARGE
OR DD 214 FORM_____

LOCATION OF LEGAL DOCUMENTS

BIRTH CERTIFICATE _____

MARRIAGE CERTIFICATE_____

DIVORCE DECREE _____

PASSPORT _____

WILL OR TRUST _____

DEEDS _____

MORTGAGES _____

TITLE TO MOTOR VEHICLES _____

HEALTH CARE DIRECTIVES _____

NAME, PHONE NO. OF ATTORNEY_____

LOCATION OF FINANCIAL RECORDS

INSURANCE POLICIES:

NAME OF COMPANY & PHONE NO. _____

LOCATION OF POLICY _____

BENEFICIARY OF POLICY _____

PENSIONS/ANNUITIES:

IF FEDERAL RETIREE: PIN NUMBER: _____

NAME OF SURVIVOR _____

SURVIVOR PIN NUMBER _____

BANK

BANK: ACCOUNT NO._____

NAME, ADDRESS OF FINANCIAL INSTITUTION

_____

LOCATION OF SAFE DEPOSIT BOX _____

LOCATION OF KEY TO BOX _____

SECURITIES

NAME AND PHONE NUMBER OF BROKER

_____

TAX RECORDS FOR PAST 3 YEARS

LOCATION _____

ACCOUNTANT: NAME, PHONE # _____

_____

WHEN TO UPDATE YOUR ESTATE PLAN

We discussed people's natural disinclination to make an estate plan until they are faced with their own mortality. Many believe that they will make just one Will and then die (maybe that's why they put off making a Will). The reality is, that most people who make a Will change it at least once before they die.

If you have an estate plan, it is important to update it when any of the following things take place:

✍ RELOCATION TO A NEW STATE OR COUNTRY

If you move within state then there is no need to change your estate plan, but if you move to another state or country, then you need to check to see whether your plan is valid in that state. Each state (and country) has its own laws relating to the inheritance of property and those laws are very different from each other. Items that are protected from a creditor in one state, may not be creditor proof in another state. Each state has its own estate tax structure. If estate taxes are high, you may need an estate plan that will minimize the impact of those taxes.

Each state has its own, unique, Law of Descent and Distribution. Who has the right to inherit your property in one state may be different from who can inherit your property in another. The rights of a spouse in a community property state are very different from those in other states. Even if you have a Will, what one state considers to be a valid Will, may be different from what another state considers to be valid. If you move to another state or country, then it is important to either educate yourself about the laws of the state, or to consult with an attorney who can assist you in reviewing your estate plan to see if that plan will accomplish your goals in that state.

✍ A SIGNIFICANT CHANGE IN THE LAW

It is important to keep up with changes in the law. You can do so by reading your daily newspaper, listening to the news on television, and/or keeping in touch with your attorney to learn if any new law will affect your estate plan. For example, Texas allows an unlimited creditor protection for the homestead. As of this writing the federal government is discussing a $100,000 limit on homestead exemptions. If the law is passed and you have significant debts, then this may impact your estate plan.

Laws relating to the inheritance of property and the way estates are probated, have remained stable over the years but tax laws are in a constant state of flux. You need to be aware of how the tax structure is being changed and how that change affects your estate plan. It is a good idea to discuss significant changes in the tax code with your accountant (or attorney) to learn how that change will affect you.

✍ A CHANGE IN RELATIONSHIP

If you get married, divorced, have a child or lose a beneficiary of your estate, then you should examine your estate plan to determine whether it needs to be revised. If your marriage is annulled or you get divorced, your final judgment of divorce may state what property belongs to each of you, however, it is important to see that title to the property is changed in accordance with that judgment. For example, if you get the house and car, then title to the house and car need to changed to your name only.

It is also important to change all of your estate planning documents, this includes, Wills, Trusts, Powers of Attorney, beneficiaries to life insurance policies, pension plans, etc.

GAMES DECEDENTS PLAY

We discussed the game of "hide and seek" some decedents play with their heirs. A variation of that game is the "wild goose chase." The decedent never updates his files, so his records are filled with all sorts of lapsed insurance policies, promissory notes of debts long since paid; brokerage statements of securities that have been sold. The family wastes time trying to locate the "missing" asset.

The best joke is to keep the key to a safe deposit box that you are no longer leasing. That will keep folks hunting for a long time!

If you do not have a wicked sense of humor, then do your family a favor and update your records on a regular basis.

Completing The Process 9

The funeral is over.

Everyone went home.

You experienced and got past the initial grief.

All the affairs of the decedent have been settled.

You even did some of the things suggested in Chapters 7 and 8 so you feel that your own affairs are now in order. But is the grieving over? Do you have closure? To use a tired expression, have you been able to "get on with your life" or do you find that you are still grieving?

And how about the children in the decedent's life? How are they taking the loss?

The death event is not over until the family finally finds peace and acceptance of the loss. This chapter deals with issues that may arise as the family goes through the grieving process.

THE GRIEVING PROCESS

Psychologists have observed that it is common for a person to go through a series of stages as part of the grieving process.   There is the initial shock of the death and often disbelief and denial:

"He can't be dead.   I just spoke to him today!"

It is common for a mourner to be angry — angry at the decedent for dying — angry at a family member for something he should or shouldn't have done — just plain angry.

Sometimes an ill person is aware of his impending death and becomes angry, as if mourning his own death. Relations with the family may become strained under the stress of the illness.   If there was an argument with the decedent, the bereaved may be left with an unresolved conflict and feelings of guilt.

Mourners often experience guilt. Many have an uneasy feeling that the death was somehow their fault. Some regret not having spent more time with the decedent. Others feel guilty because they weren't present when the decedent died.

There is grieving even when death is long expected and even welcomed. This was the case with a wife who nursed her husband at home for nine long years. Her husband suffered from debilitating strokes, a chronic heart condition, and finally failing kidneys. She often said "Some things are worse than death." But when he died, she was surprised at the depth of her emotions.

Although professionals in the fields of psychiatry and psychology have observed that guilt and anger are stages of grieving, there is no agreement about the number or composition of the stages of grieving. This is not surprising. The ways people react to death is as diverse as there are people. Some people seem not to grieve at all. Whether such people experience any stage of the grieving process may not be known even to the person himself/herself.

And there is diversity in grieving even in the same person. Each circumstance of death in one's life is different from another, so a person will grieve differently when different people in their life die. But for purposes of this discussion, we note that many people who lose someone they love report experiencing the following emotions and in the following sequence:

> ➢ initial shock, disbelief, alarm
> ➢ numbness, anger, guilt
> ➢ pining, searching for the deceased
> ➢ sadness, depression, loneliness
> ➢ recovery, acceptance of the loss, peace

COPING WITH THE LOSS

How the general population deals with the death of a loved one was investigated in 1995 by the AMERICAN ASSOCIATION OF RETIRED PERSONS ("AARP"). AARP asked National Communications Research to conduct a telephone survey of over 5,000 people aged 40 or older. Approximately one third of the respondents reported that they had experienced the loss of a close friend or family member within the past year.   Those reporting a loss were asked to describe specific   coping activities that they had engaged in since the death of their loved one.

    67% reported talking with friends and family
    16% read an article or book about how
             to cope with death
     9% received help with legal
             or practical arrangements
     5% attended a grief support group

When asked what strategies they found to be most helpful in coping with their loss:

    28% said talking with a friend or family
             member was most helpful
    24% said their religion was most helpful
    10% said knowing it was for the best
     6% said memories of the deceased
     4% reported staying busy as the best strategy.

It is interesting to note that 67% of the people who suffered a loss turned to family and friends to help them cope with the loss. Although talking with family and friends topped the list as the most commonly used strategy, only 28% reported this as being most helpful to them. Many times friends and family members want to help but they are at a loss as to what to say or do.   The next section discusses different techniques that can be used to help with the grieving process.

HELPING THE BEREAVED

Family and friends want to help the person who is grieving, but sometimes they don't know how to do it. They may feel just as helpless in dealing with the loss as does the bereaved — not knowing what to say to console those grieving.

There are no magic words, but saying you are sorry for the loss is appropriate and generally well received. Avoid platitudes such as: "It was fate." "It was God's will." "It was for the best." Especially avoid telling the bereaved that you know how he/she feels. People who suffer a great loss do not believe that anyone can understand how they feel; and they are probably correct. It is better to tell the bereaved what you are feeling:

"I was shocked when I heard of the death."

"I am so sad for you."

"I am going to really miss him."

Knowing that you share the feeling of loss is comforting to someone who is grieving.

Listening is more important than talking to the bereaved. They may need to explore the circumstances of the death — how the person died; where and when he died, etc. They may need to express what they are feeling, whether it be grief or anger. Try not to change the subject just because you are uncomfortable with the topic or with the expression of emotion.

If the bereaved wishes to reminisce about the decedent, then join in the conversation. Talk about the decedent's good qualities and the enjoyable times that you shared.

If during the funeral period, you want to do something such as prepare food or send flowers, then consider asking the bereaved for permission to do so. The family may prefer donations to a favorite charity in place of flowers. The family may have already made dinner plans for the guests. Do not make general offers of assistance. "Let me know if you need anything" is not likely to get a response even if the bereaved does need help with something. A better, more sincere, approach is a specific offer, such as, "If you need transportation, I can drive you to the cemetery."

Your assistance during the post-funeral period is more important than during the funeral period. During the funeral the bereaved is usually surrounded by family and friends and has more than ample assistance. Any offer to help at that time may not even register because the bereaved may be numb with grief — unable to comprehend what is going on around them — unable to even recall who was present at the funeral, nonetheless who offered to assist them.

Once the funeral is over and everyone has gone home, that is the time to offer support. The bereaved needs to go through a transition period and must learn to live without the presence of their loved one. In general, the more dependent the bereaved was on the decedent, the more difficult the transition. In such case, you can be most helpful if you are able to offer assistance with those tasks of daily living that the bereaved is not accustomed to performing. For example, if the decedent was the sole driver in the family, then you might help the bereaved to learn to drive or at least help find public transportation. If the decedent handled all of the family finances, you might assist the bereaved in bill paying and balancing a checkbook. If math is not your forte, help to find a bookkeeper who can assist for a reasonable fee.

But, the best thing that family and friends can do for the bereaved, is just to be there for them. As shown by the AARP survey, the specific coping activity used by the majority of the bereaved was to talk to a friend or relative. A telephone call, or a card, on a special anniversary or on a holiday will be appreciated. You can help most with a call or a visit. It is just that simple.

Also be patient with the bereaved. There is no set time to get through the grieving process. It may take considerable time for the mourner to be able to find some quality of life. If several months have passed and you are concerned that the bereaved is still not functioning well, or at least, better, then you might consider suggesting that the bereaved seek professional counseling. Try not to be judgmental when making the suggestion. Don't say "You should be feeling better by now," but rather, "I can see that you are still having a hard time getting through this difficult period. Have you considered seeing _____"

Suggest whatever is appropriate to the mourner. For example, if the mourner is a religious person, then suggest a visit with his/her religious leader. If the mourner is a social person, then suggest a support group. If the bereaved is severely depressed then a visit to a doctor or psychiatrist may be the best recommendation.

Do not expect your recommendation to be well received. The mourner may become angry or annoyed that you even made the suggestion. It may be difficult for the mourner to accept the fact that he/she needs assistance. Some people, mostly men, think it an admission of weakness to agree that they need help. They believe they should be able to "tough it out."

Some mourners may have increased their consumption of alcohol or turned to drugs in an attempt to deal with the pain that they are experiencing. If they accept your suggestion, they may need to deal with a growing addiction, in addition to the problem of overcoming the grief, and they may not be willing to do that.

Elderly people might think there is a stigma associated with any kind of counseling. They may insist "There's nothing wrong with me" fearing that you think they are unbalanced or somehow mentally defective.

Some people, especially the overachiever type, refuse to seek counseling because they perceive asking for help to be a sign of failure — an admission that they failed to work out the problem themselves. It's as if they failed "Grieving 101."

But those most resistant to a suggestion of a need for counseling are mourners who use denial as a defense mechanism. They may brush off the suggestion with "No. I'm alright" or "I'm doing a lot better." If they deny that they are having trouble getting past the grief, then they do not need to deal with the problem. If they deny that they have a problem, then they don't have the problem and that solves that!

In such cases, the timeworn adage, "You can lead a horse to water, but you can't make him drink," applies. The mourner needs to take the first step himself. You cannot take it for him. All you can do is assure the mourner (and yourself) that you have confidence that he/she can, and will, work this through.

HELPING A CHILD THROUGH THE LOSS

The first thing parents observe about their second child is how very different that child is from their first child. Parents quickly learn that each of their children is an individual, with his/her own separate response to any given situation. It is important to keep this fact in mind when trying to assist a child through the loss of a close family member or friend. Because each child is different, there is no single proper way to assist a child through a period of mourning. You can help the child most if you consider the child's background as it relates to the loss:

What is the child's relationship to the decedent?
What were the circumstances of the death?
Was it expected or was it sudden or tragic?
What is the emotional age of the child? That age may differ significantly from his/her chronological age.

As an example, consider the family of Harold and Elaine, parents of three children. Emily, the eldest child, was one of those "born old" children, wise beyond her years, sensitive and shy. Her brother John, two years her junior was the direct opposite — boisterous, immature, constantly in motion. Peter came along five years later. He was the baby of the family, a cherub, always smiling, indulged by parents and siblings.

When their paternal grandfather died, Emily was 10, John, 8 and Peter, 3. Their parents expected the death because "Gramps" had been suffering from cancer for a long time. No mention was made to the children of the serious nature of the illness, so Emily was surprised to learn of the death. She shed no tears but retreated to her room and soon became occupied with a computer game.

John and his father cried together when they were told that Gramps had died. Gramps was both kind and generous with a great sense of humor. Best of all he was never critical of John's rambunctious behavior. It seemed to John and his Dad that they lost the best friend they ever had.

Peter did not understand what was going on; but he reacted empathetically, patting John on the shoulder, and saying "Don't cry Johnny."

When it came time to go to the funeral Emily refused to go. Johnny got angry with Emily for something or another and pushed her down. She was not hurt, but she cried loudly and carried on. Peter started whining. The whole day was hard on their parents.

The next few months were equally difficult. John woke up with nightmares. Emily was sullen and withdrawn. No one mentioned the death except Peter who was full of questions: "Where's Gramps?"
  "Was he in that box?"
  "Where did they put the box?"
  "Why was everyone crying?"

Harold and Elaine were having their own problems dealing with the loss and they had no patience with the children. The family eventually got back to normal, but it might have been easier on all of them had the parents prepared the children for the dying process.

PREPARING FOR THE EVENT

Most deaths are expected. The majority of people who die are ill for several months before their death.   Children are not always aware of a family member's mortal illness so it comes as a shock to them when it happens. It might have been easier on Emily and John if their parents said something like:

> *Gramps is old and very ill. It happens that all living*
> *things, plants, animals and people, eventually die.*
> *No one knows for sure when someone will die, but*
> *it may be that because he is so old and so very sick*
> *that Gramps may die sometime within the year.*

If either child wanted to pursue the subject then that could lead to a discussion of the funeral process:

> *When someone dies in our family, all of our friends*
> *and family gather together to talk about how much*
> *we loved the person and how much we will miss*
> *having that person with us.   Later we go to the*
> *gravesite where we say prayers and our last good-byes.*

It is important for parents to explain the children's role in this process, but like most couples, Harold and Elaine never thought about, much less discussed, their children's participation in the funeral and burial service. Had her parents told Emily what to expect and what was expected of her, she might not have objected to attending the funeral.

Before discussing the matter with the child, it is important that a husband and wife explore their own views on their children's participation in a funeral and burial. They may find that they have differing views on the following issues:

What factors should determine whether a child attends the wake and/or funeral:

    ▷   custom or convenience?

    ▷   the age and emotional maturity of that child?

    ▷   the relationship of the child to the decedent?

Should the child be allowed to decide whether he/she wishes to attend the wake and/or funeral?

Should a child be allowed (or encouraged) to touch or kiss the corpse?

Should children participate in grave site ceremonies?

Should a child be encouraged or required to visit the grave site at a later date?

There are no right or wrong answers for any of the above questions.   Each family has its own set of customs and values and the answers to these questions need to conform to those customs and values. What is important is that the couple agree about what they expect of their children and then impart that expectation to their children.

The "imparting" is the difficult part.   No one likes to talk about death.   Parents have been told that they need to discuss sex with their children. They have been told that they need to discuss drugs with their children.   These are important, life threatening, issues but it is entirely possible that a child will grow to be an adult without ever having someone close to them die. So why bring up the subject?

The reason to discuss the matter is the same reason to discuss sex with your children. The sex they see on television or hear about from their friends is a reflection of societal values but perhaps not your family values. You discuss sex to impart your family values and expectations to your children. If you wish to express to your children your views on the dying process and the afterlife (or the lack of it, if that is your belief) then it is appropriate to discuss these matters when you believe the child is sufficiently mature and ready for the discussion.

Still another reason to discuss death with the child is when someone close to them is quite aged or seriously ill. If they heard that some family member is dying, they may have concerns or questions that you can answer. Most children fear the unknown and death is an unknown to them. Of course, children are aware of the fact of death almost as soon as they can speak. It is all around them. Animated characters "die" as part of a computer game. Children's cartoon movies and television shows contain death and dying scenes. A child may have a pet that dies. Children hear about people dying almost nightly on the news.

Although children are familiar with the concept of death, they do not know how they or their family will react to the death of a loved one. If the topic is discussed prior to an impending death, the child may find it comforting to know what to expect, what behavior is expected of them, and what choices they may have regarding their attendance at a wake or funeral.

AFTER THE FUNERAL

Once the funeral is over, you need to deal with your own loss. That may be a difficult process for you so you may not even notice that your child is also grieving. This was the case with Harold and Elaine. They were not aware that Emily was having a difficult time with the loss — after all she didn't even cry when she heard of the death. Had they thought about it, they may have realized that Emily was retreating into herself as a defense mechanism for dealing with the loss. Her continued sullen attitude after the funeral was a tip off that she was having difficulty getting beyond the loss.

If her parents had encouraged Emily to talk about the problem, they would have learned that she had ambivalent feelings about her grandfather. She loved him, but she felt that he favored her brothers. Gramps always played "boy" games of catch and touch football. He never took the time to get to know Emily and she resented that. Now that he was gone, there would be no opportunity for her to have a meaningful relationship with her grandfather.

People are helped most by talking with a friend or relative about their loss. The same applies to children. Emily could have profited had she been able to explore her feelings with either of her parents. Her parents might also have profited because they may have developed a closer relationship with Emily and established a pattern of open communication.

As it was, Emily never did resolve the problem. Her parents suffered her sullenness without ever a clue as to what Emily was all about. Unfortunately, this lack of communication continued as Emily grew older and ever more a closed book.

John fared better. Harold recognized that John's nightmares were related to the loss. Harold made an effort to spend more time with the boy and not to be so critical when John acted up.

As for Peter, his parents tried to answer his questions as best as they were able. Elaine had the uneasy feeling that she was not answering them "the right way." She thought she made a mistake by saying that "Gramps is now at rest" because Peter asked if Gramps was sleeping. She thought that she might have caused Peter to confuse death and sleep.

Had Elaine investigated she could have found any number of excellent publications dealing with the subject. Many funeral homes provide families with complimentary pamphlets on how to answer children's questions about death. The local library and bookstore have any number of excellent publications designed to answer questions raised by small children.

Most religious organizations offer printed material for young people that explain death from the organization's perspective. For religious families, this is a good opportunity for the family to discuss their religious beliefs as they relate to the loss of a loved one.

INTERNET RESOURCES

Many Web sites offer free publications on how to deal with the issues of death and dying. You can use your browser to locate such sites.

Today's child is computer literate. A child may, on his own, decide to seek an E-mail buddy to work through a problem the child may be having with the death. Parents need to supervise such communication because the child may be especially vulnerable at this point in his/her life.

There are Web sites that offer organized E-mail grief support groups. One such site is GriefNet. This Web site is operated by Rivendell Resources, a non-profit organization:

GriefNet   (734) 761-1960
P.O. Box 3272
Ann Arbor, MI 48106-3272
          E-mail: visibility@griefnet.org

KIDSAID is a companion Web site to GriefNet. They offer peer support groups for children who are dealing with a loss. Parental permission is required before the child is allowed to join a support group.

   http://www.griefnet.org/KIDSAID/kids2kids.html

THE TROUBLED CHILD

Most deaths are from natural causes. The death is expected and not all that difficult for the family to finally accept. The *problem death* is one that is tragic, unexpected, and/or a death that cuts short a life. More and more school officials are recognizing that the loss of a member of the school community deeply affects the student population. Many schools have adopted a policy of having school psychologists counsel the students as soon as the death occurs. They do not wait until a school child shows signs of being disturbed by the event.

It would be well for parents to adopt the same policy. Specifically, if your family suffers a problem death then consider seeking the services of a professional who is experienced in grief counseling just as soon after the death as is practicable.

A death does not always need to be a problem death to cause a problem in a child. As discussed before, if a child has unresolved issues, then that child may need professional assistance in coping with the loss. Children do not manifest grief or depression in the same way as adults, so look for changes that are atypical of the child and that do not resolve themselves within a reasonable time after the death. Consider consulting with a child psychologist if your child exhibits unusual or antisocial behavior such as:

> ‣ eating too much or too little
> ‣ destructive or aggressive behavior
> ‣ sleeping too much or too little
> ‣ misbehaving at school
> ‣ a sudden change in school performance

The red flag, signaling an immediate need for counseling, is a child who talks or writes about committing suicide. It is important to act quickly to show the child that you understand that he/she is having a rough time and that you and the doctor are going to assist the child with the problem.

There are any number of resources in the community to assist the child, from school counselors to religious organizations. The TEXAS PSYCHOLOGICAL ASSOCIATION, located in Austin, offers a free referral service for all counties of the state. You can reach them at (512) 280-4099.

For those who cannot afford private care, counties offer low-cost services on an ability to pay basis. Some religious organizations offer counseling services to their members, as well as to the general public, on a sliding scale basis.

Before seeking counseling services, it is important to schedule a physical checkup for the child. There is a chance that the problem is physiological. Some illnesses cause behavioral changes; for example, food allergies can cause aggressive behavior. Hearing or visual deficiencies can cause a child to withdraw into himself. Even infections can cause behavioral disturbances. Perhaps the child is on drugs and an examination should pick that up. All these things need to be ruled out prior to counseling.

If your child has been treated by the physician over the years, the doctor may know the child well enough to be able to offer some insight into the problem. If the checkup does not reveal a physical problem, the physician may be able to suggest the right type of treatment, i.e., psychologist or psychiatrist, and perhaps give you a referral.

CHOOSING THE RIGHT COUNSELOR

There was a film called GOOD WILL HUNTING in which a brilliant, but troubled, teenager was required, by court order, to attend counseling. The funniest part of the film was the manner in which the boy went through counselors. He deliberately alienated (and was alienated) by many doctors until he met the right one for him. Similarly, if your child needs counseling you might need to interview several counselors before you find someone with whom your child can work; someone who speaks on his/her level — someone the child can trust.

The issue of trust may create a dilemma for the parent. The child is the counselor's patient. The counselor cannot betray the child's trust by revealing what was said during treatment, yet parents need to know whether the treatment is helping the child. The counselor can, and should, disclose to the parent the diagnosis, prognosis and type of proposed treatment. The parents need to employ someone they trust to pursue the course of treatment that they determine is best for their child.

In seeking a counselor, personal references are the best avenue, although it may be difficult to find a friend or relation who has had his/her child successfully treated for a similar problem. With or without references, you need to investigate the counselor's background. What is his/her training? What percentage of the practice is devoted to children in this age group? Is the counselor experienced in working with children who are having difficulty coping with the loss of a loved one?

Interview more than one counselor before making your choice. If the child is sufficiently mature and able to cooperate in choosing the right counselor, then that is an important step forward. If not, you may need to be assertive and go with the counselor whom you trust and are most comfortable. If it turns out that there is no improvement within a few months, then you need to find another counselor. As with the student in GOOD WILL HUNTING, it may take several tries before you come upon someone who can help your child.

STRATEGIES TO COPE WITH THE LOSS

Once the person accepts the fact of death, they are past the initial phase of the grief process. Most people do very well and are able to go through the remaining stages with no overt effort on their part. Others suffer profoundly and need to find ways to get through the grieving process. If you have recently experienced a loss and are having difficulty coping with the loss then consider your own personality type and explore those strategies that might help you through.

Do you enjoy socializing with people or do you prefer solitary activities? Are you a "do-it-yourself" type of person or do you feel more at ease with someone leading you through the process?

STRATEGIES FOR THE PRIVATE PERSON

If you find socializing to be difficult, then consider non-social activities such as reading a self help book. There are many excellent publications that explore the grieving process and how to adjust to the loss. Praying or quiet meditation may offer you consolation. This may be a good time to explore different kinds of meditative techniques. You can find books on meditative techniques such as Zen or visualization in the Philosophy section of the library or bookstore. You can find books on Yoga in the exercise section.

If you are computer literate, then you can use your browser to locate an Internet support group. An anonymous friend may be the perfect confidant to help you to work through

STRATEGIES FOR THE SOCIAL MINDED

If you are a social person, then consider using those types of activities that involve a social setting, such as joining a bridge, bowling or golfing group. If your grief is too deep to concentrate on recreational activities, consider joining a support group. The power of the support group is companionship. They offer the one thing you may need most at this time — just someone to listen.

If you belong to an organized religion or a civic organization, find out whether they have a support group for people who are going through a grieving process. If your organization does not have a support group, then consider starting one yourself. It can be as simple as putting a notice in a weekly bulletin that you are holding a meeting for anyone who lost a loved one within the past year. You can hold the meeting as part of a picnic or barbecue with everyone bringing a dish for others to share. Just getting together and sharing experiences may help you and others in your organization as well.

If you do not belong to an organization, then look in the newspaper for notices of meetings of local support groups or consider joining one of the many national support groups. The following are some of the well established national groups:

FOR WIDOWED PERSONS

THEOS   (412) 471-7779
(They Help Each Other Spiritually)
322 Boulevard of the Allies, Suite 105
Pittsburgh, PA   15222-1919

THEOS is a national organization with a volunteer network of recently widowed persons. They have support chapters in many states. If you wish to establish a support group in your area, they will help you to do so.

꙳ ꙳

AARP GRIEF AND LOSS PROGRAM
WIDOWED PERSONS SERVICE   (800) 424-3410
601 E Street NW
Washington, DC 20049

AARP has support groups for widowed persons throughout the United States. They also have support groups for adults who have suffered the loss of a family member such as a parent or sibling. You can call the above number and they will let you know if there is a support group in your area.

E-mail: griefandloss@ aarp.org
Web site: www.aarp.org/griefprograms

FOR WIDOWED PARENTS

PARENTS WITHOUT PARTNERS   (800) 637-7974
401 N. Michigan Avenue
Chicago, IL 60611-6267

PARENTS WITHOUT PARTNERS is a national non-profit organization for single parents. They offer group discussions and single parent activities such as picnics and hikes. Their national headquarters can direct you to the chapter nearest you.

E-mail: pwp@sba.com
Web site: http://parentswithoutpartners.org

PET GRIEF SUPPORT SERVICES

Those who suffer the loss of a pet may experience a sense of loss similar to the loss of a close family member. Often they hesitate to turn to friends or family members (especially those who never owned a pet) believing they just wouldn't understand.

Some local Humane Societies provide a pet loss counseling service.

There is a list of pet grief counseling services for other states at
http://www.superdog.com/

BE GOOD TO YOU

People who suffer extreme grief tend to become extreme in everyday activities. They may forget to eat. Some find themselves eating all day. Some mourners develop sleep disturbances and go without sleep for long periods of time while others suffer the opposite extreme of wanting to sleep all day. If you find that your grief is affecting your physical well being, then you need to make a conscious effort to care for yourself:

✰ EAT A BALANCED NUTRITIONAL DIET

Contrary to popular taste, sugar, salt, fat and chocolate do not constitute the four basic food groups. And contrary to current food faddism, no one diet fits all. The ability to digest certain foods varies from person to person and we all have ethnic preferences. You need to learn what balance of fats, protein (meat, fish, legumes) and carbohydrates (fruit, vegetables, grains) you require to maintain your optimum weight and state of well being; and then make an effort to keep that balance in your daily diet.

✰ GET SUFFICIENT REST

There is much variation in the amount of sleep required from person to person. You know how much sleep you normally require. Try to maintain your usual, pre-loss, sleep pattern. If you are finding difficulty sleeping at night, resist the urge to sleep during the day. It is easy to reverse your days and nights. Awake all night, dozing all day, will only make you feel as if you are walking around in a fog.

✻ EXERCISE EACH DAY

Exercise can be as simple as taking a brisk 20 minute walk, however the more sustained and energetic, the greater the benefit. If you are having trouble sleeping at night, try exercising during the late afternoon and eating your main meal at lunch rather than late at night.

✻ THINK POSITIVE THOUGHTS

Make an effort to concentrate on things in your life that are right, as opposed to thoughts that make you angry or sad. This may be difficult to do. During periods of high stress, you may feel as if your mind has a mind of its own. Thoughts may race through your mind even though you'd just as soon not think them. Prayer and/or meditation may help you to reestablish discipline in your thinking process.

Eating right, getting sufficient sleep, exercising and thinking positive thoughts — most people have heard these recommendations from so many sources (doctors, psychologists, writers for health magazines, etc.) that they seem to have become a cliche. But the reason that so many professionals make these suggestions is simply that they work. Doing all these things will make you feel significantly better.

But if you feel so down that you are unable to help yourself, then you may need professional help to get you through this difficult period. Check with your health care plan to see if they will cover the cost of a visit to a psychiatrist or psychologist.

ADJUSTING TO A NEW LIFE STYLE

If you lost a member of your immediate family, then in addition to going through the stages of the grieving process, you need to go through a transition period in which you learn how to live without the decedent. The child must learn to live without the guidance of a parent. Parents may need to put their parenting behind them. The spouse must learn to live without a partner, and as a single person.

In addition to learning to live with the loss, the bereaved may need to establish a new identity. Such was the case with Claire. She and Fred were married 44 years when he died after a lengthy battle with cancer. At first Claire didn't think she could live without him. She had been a wife for so long. She had trouble thinking of herself as a single person — nonetheless being one.

Claire had difficulty accepting the fact that Fred was dead, even though she expected he would die for months before he did. She would see Fred in her dreams. Sometimes she thought she saw him sitting in his favorite chair. When Fred appeared to Claire, he looked the same as when they were first married. Sometimes she thought he was speaking to her.

What was most comforting to Claire was that Fred was smiling at her. She was relieved to know that Fred was no longer in pain and was at peace. The smile on his face was a relief to her because she feared he might be angry with her for the many times he would call out her name and she would become annoyed with him. She felt guilty that she did not have more patience as a caregiver.

Claire found herself talking to Fred especially during those times that she was undecided as to what to do. As time progressed, she began to incorporate her husband's beliefs into her own so that instead of asking herself "What should I do?" it became "This is what Fred would have done."

Eventually Claire found that she was able to function on her own. She began to re-engage with the world. She found new interests to pleasantly occupy her time. She learned how to live as a single person. She is now more self sufficient than at any other time in her life. She laments that Fred no longer visits her. She still misses him.

Claire was able to get beyond the grief. She did it on her own, though she will tell you that she did it with Fred's help.

Claire's case is not unusual. As verified by the AARP survey, most people adjust to the loss on their own, requiring only an assist from family and friends, but there is a percentage of the grieving population that will require assistance and need to seek professional grief counseling.

For those experiencing psychological problems prior to the death, the event of the death may be the precipitating factor to mental illness requiring treatment. Similarly, if a person had a drinking problem or a drug addiction before the death, the event of the death may exacerbate the addiction.

Some deaths are so violent or tragic, that even the sturdiest may be unable to resume their life without professional assistance. In the next section, we discuss ways of coping with the problem death.

THE PROBLEM DEATH

As discussed, the problem death is one that is unexpected, tragic or a death that cuts short a life. Such a death is an immediate problem in terms of the funeral, burial and estate settlement, but the most difficult problem is getting through the mourning period.

The death of a child is always a problem death. Even if the child is an adult, the parent experiences extreme grief. No one expects to outlive his or her child. In these days of a lengthening life cycle, more and more parents may come to experience such a loss. The loss may come at a time when the parent is frail or in poor health, making it all the more difficult to deal with the loss.

The only thing harder than losing an adult child is losing a young child. Nothing compares to the intensity of grief experienced by a parent when a little one dies. Some parents believe they are losing their mind. Many feel that their lives can never have meaning again. Guilt and recrimination flow, "Maybe I could have prevented it." There is even guilt for returning to ordinary living. If the parents find themselves smiling, laughing or making love they think, "How can we be doing this? How can we ever be normal again?"

The family who experiences a tragic or violent death should consider seeking professional grief counseling as soon as practicable after the death. The grief counseling can be in the format of a self-help group. Participants are able to talk and share their pain with others like themselves who understand what they are experiencing.

There are many specialized self-help groups that provide literature and support from people who have suffered a similar loss:

FOR PRENATAL OR NEONATAL DEATHS

M.E.N.D. **M**ommies **E**nduring **N**eonatal **D**eath
P.O. Box 1007   (888)-695-MEND
Coppell, TX   75019

MEND provides monthly newsletters and has a Web site that with information:.

    http://www.mend.org
    E-mail rebekah@mend.org

🦋🦋🦋🦋🦋🦋🦋🦋🦋🦋🦋🦋🦋🦋🦋🦋🦋🦋🦋🦋🦋🦋🦋🦋🦋🦋🦋🦋🦋

SHARE   (800) 821-6819
National Share Pregnancy and Infant Loss Support
St. Joseph Health Center
300 First Corporate Drive
St. Charles, MO   63012-2893

SHARE is a resource center for bereaved parents. They have support groups throughout the United States. You can call the national office for the telephone number of the support group in your state.

    http://www.nationalshareoffice.com
    E-mail share@nationalshareoffice

FOR FAMILIES OF A DECEASED CHILD

THE COMPASSIONATE FRIENDS
National Chapter: (630) 990-0010
P.O. Box 3696, Oak Brook, IL 60522
THE COMPASSIONATE FRIENDS have local chapters with volunteers (themselves bereaved parents) to accept telephone calls.

     http://www.compassionatefriends.org
                E-mail tcf_national@prodigy.com

🐦🐦🐦🐦🐦🐦🐦🐦🐦🐦🐦🐦🐦🐦🐦🐦🐦🐦🐦🐦🐦🐦🐦🐦🐦🐦🐦🐦🐦🐦🐦🐦🐦

A.G.A.S.T   (888) 774-7437
ALLIANCE OF GRANDPARENTS A SUPPORT IN TRAGEDY
P.O. Box 17281
Phoenix, AZ 85011-0281
AGAST supports grandparents, who have suffered the loss of a grandchild, with informational packets, peer contact and newsletters.

     E-mail: GRANMASIDS@AOL.COM

🐦🐦🐦🐦🐦🐦🐦🐦🐦🐦🐦🐦🐦🐦🐦🐦🐦🐦🐦🐦🐦🐦🐦🐦🐦🐦🐦🐦🐦🐦🐦🐦🐦

SIDS ALLIANCE   (800) 221-7437
SUDDEN INFANT DEATH SYNDROME ALLIANCE
1314 Bedford Avenue, Suite 210
Baltimore, MD 21208

The SIDS Alliance is a national, not-for-profit, voluntary organization. Their web site offers information and the names and E-mail addresses of chapters in all of the states.

     http//www.sidsalliance.org
                E-mail: sidsntsa@flash.net

FOR FAMILIES OF MURDERED CHILDREN

THE NATIONAL ORGANIZATION OF   (888) 818-POMC
PARENTS OF MURDERED CHILDREN, INC.
National Chapter
100 East Eighth Street, B-41
Cincinnati, OH   45202

POMC has support groups and contact people in each of the fifty states. There are five support groups in the state of Texas.   Contact the National Chapter for the group nearest you.

http://www.pomc.com
E-mail natlpomc@aol.com

FOR FAMILIES OF SUICIDES

AMERICAN ASSOCIATION OF SUICIDOLOGY (202) 237-2280
4201 Connecticut Ave. NW, Suite 408
Washington, DC   20008

The American Association of Suicidology is a not-for-profit organization that promotes education, public awareness and research for suicide prevention. It serves as a national clearinghouse for information on suicide. You can call for the number of a support group nearest you. Their Web site has the names addresses and phone number of several organizations that offer counseling for families who have lost a loved one to suicide.

http://www.suicidology.org

BUT WHAT IF I CAN'T STOP GRIEVING?

We observed that there are five stages of grieving:
shock/disbelief,
anger/guilt
searching/pining
sadness/depression
acceptance of the loss.

There is no right way to grieve. You may pass through a stage rapidly or even skip a stage. You may get hung up in one of the stages and have difficulty getting beyond that emotion. Some psychologists refer to this as "stuckness." It's something like what happened to 45-rpm phonograph records that were popular in the 1940's and 1950's.

For the benefit of the digital generation who have no experience with phonographs, the record was played by means of a needle that glided over groves of a revolving disk (the record). Sometimes the needle would get stuck in a groove and play the same sound over and over again until the annoyed listener bumped it into the next groove.

If you are stuck in one of the stages of mourning you may think the suggestions in this section to be useless in your situation because they encourage you to be proactive, i.e., to actively seek to help yourself. If you are thinking:
"I **can't** help myself. " or
"If I could help myself, I wouldn't have this problem," then the first thing you need to understand, and accept, is that you have no other choice but to help yourself. The pain exists within you and nowhere else. Because the pain is internal and unique to you, only you can ease that pain. This does not mean that no one can help you to deal with the pain. It just means that you need to be interactive with the healing process; and in particular, you need to take the first step.

What is that first step? To answer that question you need to identify those areas of your life with which you are having difficulty. It might help to make a list of all of the things that are bothering you. Once you compose the list, look at the last item on the list. If you are like most people, you will initially avoid thinking about what is really troubling you. It may take the last item on the list for you to admit to yourself what is really causing the problem.

Once you identify the problem, the identification itself should suggest the solution. For example, suppose you find the holidays unbearable, then a solution may be to change your holiday routine. Instead of wearing yourself out shopping for gifts, use the money to treat yourself to a boat cruise. Tell everyone that this year you are taking a holiday from the holidays. You may find that people are just as tired of exchanging gifts as you are and that they gladly welcome the change.

If your problem is being lonely, then your solution will involve companionship. How you attain that companionship will depend on your personality. If you are lonely, but not a social person, consider adopting a pet. If you are civic minded, then you may find companionship as a volunteer for community activities. If you are physically active, then perhaps you can take up a new sport or even pick up a sport that you used to enjoy at an earlier time in your life. If you enjoy sports but are not in the best shape, perhaps you can coach children's team sports.

If your problem is that you are severely depressed, then the solution will involve medical and/or psychological methods of lifting the depression. If you decide to ask for medical assistance, you need to continue to be interactive. You cannot stand passively by saying "Now heal me." Pharmaceutical hyperbole notwithstanding, there is no magic pill. An antidepressant may help you to gain control of yourself, but you still need to work through the grief.

If you feel that you have tried it all and you still are unable to find peace and contentment in your life, then you need to ask the hard question:
   "What is it about mourning that I really enjoy?"
Strange question? Not really.

You may enjoy thinking of your loved one even if the thought gives you as much pain as pleasure. You may think that if you stop mourning then you truly lose the decedent. If that's the case, then compartmentalize your grief, that is, set aside a special time of the day to actively think about and/or grieve for your loved one and the rest of the day not to grieve or even think about the decedent.

Actively plan the grieving compartment of your day. You may wish to have a grieving routine, perhaps visit the grave site once a week; or quietly spend 15 minutes a day looking at pictures of the decedent or writing down your memories of the happy times you had together. If you have been discussing your grief with family or friends, restrict such talks to specific times, perhaps on the decedent's birthday, or on the anniversary of his death.

Set aside as much time each day as you believe you need to mourn, but here is the hard part — you need to exercise self restraint not to mourn, nor talk about, nor even think of the decedent during any other part of the day. If your mind wanders back to the sadness and loneliness of the loss, postpone it. Say to yourself, "Hold that thought till my next grieving compartment."

If you are speaking to someone, do not mention the decedent or how you are feeling about the loss until your scheduled grieving talk with that person. If the subject comes up during a conversation, then change the subject by saying "We'll talk about that later."

Hopefully you will find the pain of your loss to lessen over time, in frequency and/or intensity.

It isn't so much that time heals; it is more that you learn to heal yourself over time.

Glossary

ADMINISTRATION The *administration* of a Probate Estate is the management and settlement of the decedent's affairs. There are different types of administration. See *Ancillary Administration* and *Independent Administration.*

ADVANCE DIRECTIVE An *Advance Directive* is a Health Care Directive made by someone (the principal) in the presence of witnesses or a written, notarized statement in which the principal gives directions about the health care he/she wishes to receive. See *Medical Power of Attorney* and *Directive to Physician*.

AFFIANT An *affiant* is someone who signs an affidavit and swears that it is true in the presence of a Notary Public or person with authority to administer an oath.

AFFIDAVIT An *affidavit* is a written statement of fact made by someone voluntarily and under oath, in the presence of a notary public or someone who has authority to administer an oath.

AGENT An *agent* is someone who is authorized by another (the principal) to act for or in place of the principal.

ANATOMICAL GIFT An *anatomical gift* is the donation of all or part of the body of the decedent for a specified purpose, such as transplantation or research.

ANCILLARY ADMINISTRATION An *ancillary administration* is a probate procedure that aids or assists the original (primary) probate proceeding. Ancillary administration is conducted in another state to determine the beneficiary of the decedent's property located within that state.

ANNUITANT   An *annuitant* is someone who is entitled to receive payments under an annuity contract.

ANNUITY An *annuity* is the right to receive periodic payments (monthly, quarterly) either for life or for a number of years.

ASSET An *asset* is anything owned by someone that has a value, including personal property (jewelry, paintings, securities, cash, motor vehicles, etc.) and real property (condominiums, vacant lots, acreage, residences, etc.)

ATTESTING WITNESS An *attesting witness* to a Will is someone who signs the Will, at the request of the person making the Will, for the purpose of proving that the will is valid, i.e., that the person who made the Will did sign it, and did so on his own free will.

BENEFICIARY A *beneficiary* is one who benefits from the acts of another person. In this book, we refer to a beneficiary as one who inherits a gift from the decedent.

CLAIM A *claim* against the decedent's estate is a demand for payment.   To be effective, the claim must be filed with the Probate court within the time limits set by law.

CODICIL A *codicil* to a Will is a supplement or an addition to a Will that changes certain parts of the Will.

COLUMBARIUM A *columbarium* is a vault with niches (spaces) for urns that contain the ashes of cremated bodies.

COMMON LAW MARRIAGE A *common law marriage* is one that is entered into without a state marriage license nor any kind of official marriage ceremony. A common law marriage is created by an agreement to marry, followed by the two living together as man and wife. See Informal Marriage.

COMMUNITY PROPERTY Certain states (Arizona, California, Idaho, Louisiana, Nevada, New Mexico, Texas, Washington, Wisconsin) have laws stating that property acquired by husband or wife, or both, during their marriage is *community property* and is owned equally by both of them (see separate property).

CREMAINS The word *cremains* is an abbreviation of the term *cremated remains*. It is also referred to as the *ashes* of a person who has been cremated.

DECEDENT The *decedent* is the person who died.

DESCENDANT A *descendant* of the decedent is someone from a later generation, such as the decedent's child, grandchild, great-grandchild. The Texas Rules of Descent and Distribution include adopted children as a descendant of the decedent.

DEVISE A *devise* is a gift of real property (land, condominium, etc.) made by means of a Will.

DIRECTIVE TO PHYSICIANS *Directive to Physicians and Family or Surrogates* is a Health Care Directive that gives instructions about whether life support systems should be applied in the event that the person who signs Directive is terminally ill and unable to speak for himself. In some states this is called a Living Will.

DISTRIBUTEE A *distributee* of the decedent's estate is someone who is entitled to inherit the personal property of a decedent who died without a Will.

DISTRIBUTION The *distribution* of a trust estate or of a Probate Estate is the giving to the beneficiary that part of the estate to which the beneficiary is entitled.

ESTATE A person's *estate* is all of the property (both real and personal property) owned by that person. A person's estate is also referred to as his *taxable estate* because all of the decedent's assets must be included when determining whether any Estate taxes are due when the person dies. Compare to *Probate Estate*.

FIDUCIARY A *fiduciary* is one who holds property in trust for another or one who acts for the benefit of another.

GRANTEE The *grantee* of a deed (also called the party of the second part) named in a deed is the person who receives title to the property from the grantor.

GRANTOR A *grantor* is someone who transfers property. The grantor of a deed, (also called the party of the first part), is the person who transfers property to a new owner (the *grantee*). The grantor of a trust is someone who creates the trust and then transfers property into the trust. Also see *settlor*.

HEALTH CARE AGENT A *Health Care Agent* is a person appointed by someone (the principal) under a Durable Health Care Power of Attorney to make health care decisions for the Principal in the event that the Principal is too ill to speak for himself.

HEIR   An *heir* is someone who is entitled to inherit the decedent's property in the event that the decedent dies without a Will. This definition includes the surviving spouse and the state of Texas, if the decedent had no surviving relative.

HOMESTEAD   The *homestead* is the dwelling that is owned, and occupied, in the state of Texas, as the owner's principal residence.

INDEPENDENT ADMINISTRATION   *Independent Administration* is a probate procedure that is conducted by the Personal Representative with minimal court supervision.

INDIGENT   An person who is *indigent* is one who is poor, destitute and without funds.

INFORMAL MARRIAGE   An *Informal Marriage* is similar to a common law marriage in that the couple never applied for a marriage license, nor had their marriage solemnized by a ceremony. An Informal Marriage is valid in the state of Texas provided a man and woman agreed to be married, then live together in the state of Texas as husband and wife, and hold themselves out as being married.

INTESTATE   *Intestate* means not having a Will or dying without a Will. *Testate* is to have a Will or dying with a Will.

IRREVOCABLE CONTRACT   An *irrevocable* contract is a contract that cannot be revoked, withdrawn, or cancelled by any of the parties to that contract.

KEY MAN INSURANCE   *Key man insurance* is an insurance policy designed to protect a company from economic loss in the event that an important employee of the company becomes disabled or dies.

LEGALESE *Legalese* is the special vocabulary used by attorneys to draft legal documents. Many consider legalese to be unnecessarily complex and incomprehensible.

LETTERS OF ADMINISTRATION *Letters of Administration* is a document, issued by the Probate court, giving the person who is appointed as Administrator, authority to take possession of and to administer the estate of the decedent.

LETTERS TESTAMENTARY *Letters Testamentary* is a document issued by the Probate court to the Executor of the decedent's Will giving authority to take possession of and to administer the estate of the decedent.

LIFE ESTATE A *life estate* interest in real property is the right to possess and occupy that property for so long as the holder of the life estate lives.

LITIGATION *Litigation* is the process of carrying on a lawsuit, i.e., to sue for some right or remedy in a court of law.

LIVING WILL See *Directive To Physicians*.

MEDICAID *Medicaid* is a public assistance program jointly sponsored by the federal and state government to provide medical care for people with low income.

MEDICAL POWER OF ATTORNEY A *Medical Power of Attorney* is a document that appoints someone (an *Agent*) to make medical decisions for the person who signs the document (the *Principal*) in the event that the Principal later becomes too ill to make his own medical decisions.

NEXT OF KIN   *Next of kin* has two meanings in law: *next of kin* can refer to a person's nearest blood relation or it can refer to those people (not necessarily blood relations) who are entitled to inherit the property of the decedent if the decedent died without a will.

PERJURY *Perjury* is lying under oath. The false statement can be made as a witness in court or by signing an Affidavit. Perjury is a criminal offense.

PERSONAL PROPERTY *Personal property* is all property owned by a person that is not real property (real estate). It includes cars, stocks, house furnishings, jewelry, etc.

PERSONAL REPRESENTATIVE   The *Personal Representative* is someone (the Administrator or Executor) appointed by the Probate court to settle the decedent's estate and to distribute whatever is left to the proper beneficiary.

PER STIRPES   A *per stirpes* distribution is a method of dividing inherited property such that if one of the heirs dies before the decedent dies, then his share goes to his descendants. If the deceased heir had no descendants, then the property is divided among the surviving heirs.

POWER OF ATTORNEY A *Power of Attorney* is a document that appoints an Agent to act for or on behalf of the person who signs the document (the Principal). The Power of Attorney states those things that the Agent can do on behalf of his Principal.

PREDECEASED SPOUSE   The decedent's *predeceased spouse* is someone who was married to the decedent and who died before the death of the decedent.

PRE-NUPTIAL AGREEMENT   A *pre-nuptial agreement* (also known as an *antenuptial agreement*) is an agreement made prior to marriage whereby a couple determines how their property is to be managed during their marriage and how their property is to be divided should one die, or they later divorce.

PROBATE   *Probate* is a court procedure in which a court determines the existence of a valid Will and then supervises the distribution of the Probate Estate of the decedent. In the absence of a valid Will, the court determines the proper heirs according to state law of Descent and oversees the Administration of the estate.

PROBATE ESTATE   The *Probate Estate* is that part of the decedent's estate that is subject to probate. It includes property that the decedent owned in his name only. It does not include property that was jointly with rights of survivorship. It does not include property held "in trust for" or "for the benefit of" someone.

REAL PROPERTY   *Real property,* also known as *real estate,* is land and anything permanently attached to the land such as buildings and fences.

REPARATION   *Reparation* is money paid to make up for an injury or wrongdoing.

RESIDUARY BENEFICIARY   A *residuary beneficiary* is a beneficiary named in a Will who is to receive all or part of whatever is left of the Probate Estate once all gifts specified in the Will are made and once the decedent's bills, taxes and costs of probate have been paid.

RESIDUARY ESTATE   A *residuary estate* is that part of a probate estate that is left after all expenses and costs of administration have been paid and specific gifts have been distributed.

SEPARATE PROPERTY   In Texas, the term *separate property* means property that is owned by a married person in his/her own right. It includes property the person owned prior to marriage, as well as gifts and inheritances the person during the marriage, and also monies received as a result of a personal injury.

SETTLOR   A *settlor* is someone who furnishes property that is placed in a trust. If the Settlor is also the creator of the trust, then the Settlor is also referred to as the Grantor.

SPENDTHRIFT TRUST   A *Spendthrift Trust* is a trust created to provide monies for the living expenses of a beneficiary, and at the same time protect the monies from being taken by the creditors of the beneficiary.

STATUTE OF LIMITATION   A *statute of limitation* is a federal or state law that sets maximum time periods for taking legal action. Once the time set out in the statute passes, no legal action can be taken.

SUMMARY PROCEDURE   *Summary Procedure* is a short, simple probate procedure designed to settle small estates.

SURETY ON A BOND   The *surety on a bond* for probate procedures is usually an insurance company who will pay the beneficiaries of the estate money, in the event that the Decedent's Representative fails to do his job properly.

TENANCY BY THE ENTIRETY   A *Tenancy by the Entirety* is the name of property that is held by husband and wife. It has the same legal effect as a joint tenancy with rights of survivorship.

TENANCY IN COMMON   *Tenancy in common* is a form of ownership such that each tenant owns his/her share without any claim to that share by the other tenants. Unlike a joint tenancy, there is no right of survivorship. Once a tenant in common dies, his/her share belongs to the tenant's estate and not to the remaining owners of the property.

TESTATE   *Testate* means having a Will or dying with a Will.

TITLE INSURANCE   *Title Insurance* is a policy issued by a title company after searching title to the property. The policy insures the accuracy of its search against any claim of a defective title.

TRUST AGREEMENT A *trust agreement* is document in which someone (the Grantor or Settlor) creates a trust and appoints a trustee to manage property placed into the trust. The usual purpose of the trust is to benefit persons or charities named by the Grantor as beneficiaries of the trust.

TRUSTEE A *trustee* is a person, or institution, who accepts the duty of caring for property for the benefit of another.

UNDUE INFLUENCE   *Undue influence* is pressure or persuasion that overpowers a person's free will so that the dominated person is not acting intelligently or voluntarily.

WAIVER   A *waiver* is the intentional and voluntary giving up of a known right.

WARRANTY DEED   A *warranty deed* is a deed in which someone (the Grantor) transfers the property to another (the Grantee) and guarantees good title, i.e., the Grantor guarantees that he has the right to transfer the property, and that no one else has any right to the property.

INDEX

E

EMBALMING   8, 9

ESTATE
Administration   25
Plan   171, 213
Probate   105, 141
Taxable   36, 186
Update   223

EXECUTOR   25, 60, 70

EXEMPT PROPERTY   84, 85

F

FAMILY ALLOWANCE   86, 89, 120

FEDERAL RETIREE   30,219

FEDERAL STATUTES (See Statutes)

FEDERAL TRADE COMMISSION
FTC Ruling 453.3(b)(ii)   11
FTC Ruling 453.4   9
FTC Ruling 453.5   9

FIDUCIARY   60

FINANCIAL RECORDS   53

FUNERAL
Arrangements   8, 158
Director   8
Expenses   74, 89
Prearranged   7
Preneed   156-160
Problem   17

G

GIFT TAX   36, 182

GIFT TO MINOR   173, 190, 198

GOV'T PENSIONS   30, 219

GRANTEE   98, 101, 178

GRANTOR
of deed   101
of trust   37, 184

GRIEVING   228

GUARDIANSHIP   196, 197, 206

H

HEALTH CARE AGENT   166

HEALTH CARE DIRECTIVE   165

HEALTH INSURANCE   45-47
Coverage spouse   46, 47

HOLOGRAPHIC WILL   116

HOMEOWNER'S ASSOC.   44

HOMESTEAD
Capital Gains Exclusion   35
Creditor Protection   84
Gift Of   180
Tax Exemption   35, 181
Transfer   180

I

IF I DIE FILE   220

INCAPACITATED   203-205

INCOME TAX
Final return   33, 125
Records   60
Refund   125

144 LAWS ARE REFERENCED IN
When Someone Dies In Texas

Each state has its own set of laws relating to the settlement of a person's estate. The laws referenced in this book are very different from the laws of any other state. The author is in the process of "translating" *When Someone Dies* for the remaining states; that is, writing a book that incorporates the laws of the state into a book that describes how to settle the affairs of a decedent in that state. Arizona, California, Florida, Illinois, New York and Texas are in print. The following books are scheduled for release by September, 2000:

When Someone Dies in Alabama
When Someone Dies In Colorado
When Someone Dies In Georgia
When Someone Dies In Maryland
When Someone Dies In Massachusetts
When Someone Dies In Michigan
When Someone Dies In Mississippi
When Someone Dies In New Jersey
When Someone Dies In Ohio
When Someone Dies In Pennsylvania
When Someone Dies In North Carolina
When Someone Dies In Virginia
When Someone Dies In Washington

To order any of these books call (800) 824-0823 to check whether the book is available at this time.

BOOK ORDER

MAIL ORDER: EAGLE PUBLISHING COMPANY OF BOCA
4199 N. DIXIE HWY. #2
BOCA RATON, FL 33431
TELEPHONE ORDER (800) 824-0823 FAX ORDER: (561) 338-0823
INTERNET ORDER: www.eaglepublishing.com

SHIP TO: NAME _____

ADDRESS: _____

METHOD OF PAYMENT: CHECK ☐

☐ VISA   ☐ MASTER CARD   ☐ DISCOVER   ☐ AMER. EXP.

☐☐☐☐☐ ☐☐☐☐☐ ☐☐☐☐☐ ☐☐☐☐

EXPIRATION DATE _____

PAPER BACK $25   HARD COVER $32
(Price includes shipping and handling)

	QUANTITY	AMOUNT
When Someone Dies In Alabama		
When Someone Dies In Arizona		
When Someone Dies in California		
When Someone Dies In Florida		
When Someone Dies In Georgia		
When Someone Dies In Illinois		
When Someone Dies In Indiana		
When Someone Dies In Maryland		
When Someone Dies In Massachusetts		
When Someone Dies In Michigan		
When Someone Dies In Minnesota		
When Someone Dies In Mississippi		
When Someone Dies In New Jersey		
When Someone Dies In New York		
When Someone Dies In North Carolina		
When Someone Dies In Ohio		
When Someone Dies In Pennsylvania		
When Someone Dies In Tennessee		
When Someone Dies In Texas		
When Someone Dies in Virginia		
When Someone Dies in Washington		
	TOTAL	

When Someone Dies In Texas